"Grounded in a profound love for God, *Becoming* ᴄᴏme opens doors for its readers into a deeper relationship with the ultimate, divine, first host, as well as with the diverse world we get to serve. Thanks to Laura Baghdassarian Murray's insightful blend of Scripture, story, and spiritual practices, you'll gain what you need to meet others' (and your!) deepest longings for belonging."

Kara Powell, chief of leadership formation at Fuller Seminary and coauthor of *Future-Focused Church*

"In *Becoming a Person of Welcome*, spiritual director Laura Baghdassarian Murray takes readers far beyond the topic of entertaining guests in her exploration of Christian hospitality. In establishing 'welcome' as an approach to others, she expands the context of hospitality from invitations to formal dining rooms with lavish spreads and takes it to the office, the grocery line, the airport, the café, and the street. In doing so, she helps readers envision how we can carry out and express hospitality—rooted in God's movement toward us—in all our daily encounters. What a good word!"

Sandra Glahn, seminary professor and author of *Nobody's Mother*

"An authentic posture of hospitality is difficult to nurture these days. A flurry of activity in a culture of distraction teaches us non-presence, and this often keeps us from truly seeing and welcoming others. In her book *Becoming a Person of Welcome*, Laura Baghdassarian Murray encourages us to do the important work of fostering our own spirit of hospitality. Through personal stories and the brilliant examples of Jesus as our guide in the Gospels, Laura points us to the how and the why of hospitality. Read this book and become a person of welcome."

Gem and Alan Fadling, founders of Unhurried Living and authors of *What Does Your Soul Love?*

"*Becoming a Person of Welcome* invites readers into a transformative journey of embracing true hospitality. Laura Baghdassarian Murray offers a profoundly inspiring and reflective exploration into what it means to welcome others and oneself with the grace of Jesus. Essential reading for any leader, especially within the Christian community, this book is both a deep dive and a call to embody the warmth and openness that define meaningful connection."

Wil McCall, president and CEO of Dallas Leadership Foundation

"Laura Baghdassarian Murray doesn't just write about hospitality—she lives it. *Becoming a Person of Welcome* beautifully reimagines Christian hospitality not as a curated event but as a way of being with others that reflects the loving hospitality of God. With wisdom and grace, Laura provides accessible guidance in spiritual practices that cultivate radical presence."

David Wu, founder and executive director of Mosaic Formation

"Throughout history, the people of God have found themselves in seasons when they are deeply rooted and seasons when they were wandering and without a place of belonging. Hospitality is indeed a spiritual discipline that is at the very heart of Christian vocation and the Christian journey. How we make space for others seems to have profound implications on how we make space for God. *Becoming a Person of Welcome* is a rich, personal, heartfelt, and thoughtful resource that walks us through both the heart and the practice of Christian hospitality. It is as if Laura Baghdassarian Murray is personally accompanying you through a guided retreat."

David C. Wang, Cliff and Joyce Penner Chair for the Formation of Emotionally Healthy Leaders and associate professor of spiritual formation and psychology at Fuller Theological Seminary

"Many hear the word *hospitality* and think of a home-cooked meal in the dining room of a large house filled with people, or some other place of meeting. Laura Baghdassarian Murray argues for a slight modification of the understanding of hospitality, to a focus on people instead of on space. Humans, created for relationships with God and with people, can express and receive hospitality anywhere. Thus, when we are welcomed into the lives of others and have the privilege of welcoming them into ours, we experience hospitality through the gift of presence. I highly recommend this book."

Glenn R. Kreider, professor of theological studies at Dallas Theological Seminary

"Laura Baghdassarian Murray's writing is equal parts soothing and challenging. In an age when fear is on the rise and home can feel hard to find, I am grateful for her careful attention to spiritual practices as the way forward. In this, *Becoming a Person of Welcome* acts as a gentle guide for how we might do the inner (and communal) work that's so critical as we seek to embody Jesus' call to welcome the neighbor and stranger alike."

Michaela O'Donnell, author of *Make Work Matter* and the Mary and Dale Andringa Executive Director Chair at the Max De Pree Center for Leadership at Fuller Theological Seminary

"This book is a conversation. As a warm and wise spiritual guide, Laura Baghdassarian Murray sits next to us, sharing her stories and inviting us to share ours. Through stories and insights, she brings us gently into a dialogue with ourselves and with the Spirit as we consider what a life of hospitality and welcome might look like for us. Her writing is easy to read and practical to apply but reflects the depth of someone who lives a life that is both hospitable and contemplative. Read with a pen, a journal, and a curious heart, and you'll find more than you imagined."

Trisha Taylor, coauthor of *The Leader's Journey*

THE SPIRITUAL PRACTICE OF HOSPITALITY

BECOMING

A PERSON OF

WELCOME

LAURA BAGHDASSARIAN MURRAY

FOREWORD BY TOD BOLSINGER

ivp

An imprint of InterVarsity Press
Downers Grove, Illinois

InterVarsity Press
P.O. Box 1400 | Downers Grove, IL 60515-1426
ivpress.com | email@ivpress.com

InterVarsity Press® is the publishing division of InterVarsity Christian Fellowship/USA®. For more information, visit intervarsity.org.

All Scripture quotations, unless otherwise indicated, are taken from The Holy Bible, New International Version®, NIV®. Copyright © 1973, 1978, 1984, 2011 by Biblica, Inc.™ Used by permission of Zondervan. All rights reserved worldwide. www.zondervan.com. The "NIV" and "New International Version" are trademarks registered in the United States Patent and Trademark Office by Biblica, Inc.™

While any stories in this book are true, some names and identifying information may have been changed to protect the privacy of individuals.

The publisher cannot verify the accuracy or functionality of website URLs used in this book beyond the date of publication.

Cover design: Faceout Studio
Interior design: Jeanna Wiggins
Cover images: Sunburst 1289213700 / Getty Images and lamp 97222864 © CSA Images
      via Getty Images

ISBN 978-1-5140-1194-2 (print) | ISBN 978-1-5140-1195-9 (digital)

Printed in the United States of America ∞

Library of Congress Cataloging-in-Publication Data
A catalog record for this book is available from the Library of Congress.

31   30   29   28   27   26   25 | 12   11   10   9   8   7   6   5   4   3   2   1

To all the welcomers,

may your heart take courage and

not grow weary in doing good.

CONTENTS

FOREWORD

Tod Bolsinger

I WAS WALKING INTO CHURCH SERVICES a week or so after Christmas and did an odd thing. At least it was odd for me.

I changed pews. I didn't sit in "my" seat.

To be clear, I don't think of myself as a person who "has a regular pew." As a pastor, I often made playful fun of my congregants who always gravitated toward the same place in the sanctuary. But the truth is, that I sit—reflexively, unthinkingly, almost without noticing what I am doing—in the same exact spot every week.

Usually, we are walking in a couple of minutes late, often having rushed from the subway, trying hard not to miss too much. It's easier to unconsciously gravitate to the same pew, strip off coats and scarves, and try to catch up with the liturgy if you don't have to navigate trying to find a new place to sit.

While it may be an unconscious response now, it was—in the beginning—a very deliberate choosing. The sanctuary of the church we attend—and love—in New York City is an older cathedral that has very narrow pews, poor sight lines, and is dimly lit. Even with little more than one hundred people in attendance,

it is often still hard to find a good seat that doesn't leave you straining your neck to see the officiant in front.

So, most of us regulars have found "their" pew, where they tend to settle in each week in the hope that the newcomers that we are always trying to welcome won't inadvertently sit in front of us and block the view that we have worked so hard to procure over many months of trying out different sanctuary seats.

But, on this particular day, my wife, Beth, and I were walking into church a-few-minutes-later-than-our-usual-few-minutes late and I went immediately to our pew like I always do and then abruptly stopped and moved one pew up, all while wrestling out of my winter coat. I heard Beth chuckle curiously behind me as we slipped into the slightly different place and after we got situated, she nudged me and shrugged to ask why.

I nodded to a woman who was sitting in the pew behind our usual spot. "I didn't want to block her view." Beth was satisfied and joined in with the prayers not even realizing that she had just witnessed a little moment of my own sanctification. In the rush of the morning, when I am most likely to do what I always do, I had stopped and noticed that my regular routine would put a bit of a burden on another person and I did something just a little differently.

Later on, as we rode the subway home, it hit me that I had spent the early hours of that Sunday morning reading the book you are holding. I had let Laura Murray be my literary spiritual director and put a concept into my mind that shaped my actions without my even being aware of it.

When I moved from my pew, I was, in Laura's words, "embodying a posture of welcome." I was practicing hospitality in a church pew and I was being changed—at least a little bit—more into the likeness of the Lord who had long ago welcomed me into the embrace of his love.

This book will challenge your ideas of hospitality and delight you with the incredibly down-to-earth ways that you too can begin to take on a "posture" that is more like Jesus. It is winsome, and honest, filled with stories that will take you to dinner tables and board meetings and every day interactions with neighbors. It is both a practical guide and a prophetic nudge and is the kind of book that you will find yourself quoting to others, thinking that they were your own thoughts to begin with. It invites you to take small steps of embodying empathy, compassion, and grace and understands just how awkward that can feel at first.

In that way, this book on hospitality is itself a most hospitable book. And I dare say that if you read this book slowly and make its message a prayer for your own transformation, you will soon find yourself standing with others in a completely different way.

You may even find yourself giving up "your pew" too.

THE POSTURE YOU TAKE

FAMILY AND FRIENDS WELCOMED them to a foreign land. My parents were the first of their families to move across the world to gain access to opportunity, education, and a different life. The United States was a welcoming country for those who had the option and means to make the trip.

They traveled with others, friends who were also making the bold leap. My dad considered New York, where my aunt lived, but chose to settle in Texas's warmer climate. He and his friends started in small apartments, and soon their families journeyed over. My parents chose to leave the familiarity of Tehran for a foreign land. They already knew what it was to be foreigners in a land that was not their own as they were Armenians living in Iran. In the United States they were welcomed to live, to learn, and to become part of the people.

While my parents had the choice, many do not. People often enter foreign lands without agency or voice. Think of refugees, foster care children, or slaves; or those for whom home has changed due to divorces, remarriages, or deaths. Such people come against their wills, at the mercy of others, and without the security of an expected welcome. These are not choices made with agency but consequences of another's choices. These people don't choose to change their home; home is changed for them.

We live in a world filled with fear and uncertainty, where places of home are hard to find. We get lost in stories told from a distance and believe the filtered social media images. We suffer the consequences of others' decisions on both personal and global scales, and we withdraw in order to find safety in that which is closest to us. In this type of world, we need places and people of welcome. We need to take love, security, and hope to the stretches of our cities and expanses of our lands. And who better than those of us who know the love, security, and hope of a home in God?

Our home with God is the welcome that is always offered to us—the home that never leaves and will always be with us. We have a God who, like a loving parent, created a space and place for us, giving us boundaries to protect us and purposes worth pursuing. This God became like us in Jesus, who walked in our world and loved it. And we have been given the Holy Spirit to be with us forever. This means that we Christians have a God who created home, moves toward us in Jesus, and lives with us. We are always home in God. We may stumble or even lose our way at times, but we can always come back home. And it is up to us to continue to remain in God and to replicate God's welcome wherever we go.

Becoming a person of welcome starts with God, and it continues through us. Welcome isn't only found in a place; it is primarily found in people. And if it is found in people, then it can be carried from hospitals to hotels, from offices to orphanages, and from the least to the greatest. As people of welcome, we can take God's welcome wherever we go. How do we do this? Through the practice of hospitality.

THE POSTURE OF HOSPITALITY

Welcome was intrinsic in my family. It was not only a spiritual practice, but our everyday posture toward the world—there was always a guest to welcome, and everyone stopped to welcome the guest. For us, this looked like steeped tea, pastries, and fruit always at the ready. It didn't matter the time of day guests would arrive; such items were available at all times, as if by magic. We were prepared to receive guests fluidly, whether unannounced or by a formal invitation. Moreover, this way of being radiated outward from our home. My mom poured out generosity by providing meals for those living on the streets. At restaurants, my dad would always look to pay for the entire meal, no matter who was there. One Thanksgiving, when we were all adults, we had so much leftover food that we immediately started packing individual meals for those in need. We never stopped to talk about whether we would be hospitable or not. We just did it.

This posture of hospitality carries the welcome we have in God to those we encounter in our days. It shows up in how we carry ourselves and how we respond to those around us. It shows up when our eyes have been trained to see the loneliness of another and show friendship. It shows up when our hearts are soft in compassion toward the stranger at the store. It shows up when we pause our agendas for the day for even a few moments to be present to others.

Living into this posture takes practice, awareness, surrender, and action. Think of how we commit to being stronger physically. We have to work out regularly, monitor our food intake, and spend less time sitting on the sofa. Such changes take time and action. When we stay the course, we don't usually see immediate results; but over time, we find to our delight that we are stronger than we once were and have more energy for the day. If we cultivate a posture of welcome this way, we will find stores of unexpected generosity, welcome, patience, and love.

So how do we start to work toward this posture? We begin with reflecting on our actions. Self-reflection can be uncomfortable and acutely helpful. It offers us a starting point in reality. As a spiritual director, I encourage my directees to see everyday parts of life as a chance to look in a mirror. Below are a few actions and habits that you might not be used to seeing in a mirror. Taking a thoughtful look at these attributes can help us grow in self-reflection and awareness. No judgment involved—simply awareness.

MIRRORS

Mirror one: Movement.
"We didn't block off the row for Communion. Should we make the congregants move?"

I heard these words in the middle of a worship service from the head usher and a pastoral colleague. Our other colleague was in the middle of his sermon; he could see the little bit of commotion in the front row, but he kept on preaching.

Our building was under construction, so we had pivoted to new worship services and spaces. But with all the pivots, we missed a detail. This detail would affect the entire congregation of over five hundred people during Communion, so we needed to make a call fast.

Our staff whispered several options to each other. One option was to move everyone in the Communion row to different seats, right in the middle of the service. Nope. That was not going to happen. That was the least hospitable action and most disruptive action.

There was another option. We could extend hospitality by allowing the congregants to remain. Instead of moving the people, we could ask the Communion leaders to change the plan. We knew someone was going to be made uncomfortable, so we wanted to ask our leaders to make that shift. The leaders would do the moving. We made it happen. To this day, our church serves Communion in this adapted way, with roots in a moment of crisis and a choice of hospitality. We never know when disruptions will happen, when chances for hospitality will arise, and when we will need to move. Paying attention to how we move—asking whether we move toward hospitality or away from it—is an opportunity for self-reflection.

Mirror two: Limited sight.

In one spiritual direction session, my directee Lori came face to face with a spiritual predicament. She said, "God is calling me to practice more hospitality, but I don't know how. I am a single woman, and my apartment is my safe place. I have worked hard to have one safe place in my life, and I can't let a stranger in. My friend lives in a huge house up the hill, leaving her door unlocked for anyone to come in. I'm not going to do that. How can I practice hospitality when I have a small apartment, always lock my doors, and I don't feel safe letting in a stranger?"

Her concerns were legitimate and wise, and she strongly desired to live like Jesus. Why would God ask her to do something that she couldn't put into practice?

Like all of us, Lori wanted to obey God yet couldn't see how. In our session, we explored a series of questions that would help her redefine hospitality. We focused on how she could learn to live toward a posture of welcome in spaces other than a large home.

The next day, she sent me an audio text: "Laura, you will never guess what happened!" She told me how she had practiced hospitality with a stranger on a walk with her dog. She then had several more opportunities to extend hospitality. She was elated and felt great freedom to live like Jesus while permitting her home to be a safe place.

Lori had found a way to take hospitality wherever she went. In spiritual direction, she was able to look into a mirror and see her limited sight. She was able to expand her vision of hospitality: from the limited perspective that it required a big house with unlocked doors to the expansive perspective that hospitality could take place as she walked through her neighborhood.

Limited perspectives on hospitality are common. Think of the limited views that hospitality can only really occur in beautiful homes, or that hospitality is only a woman's job, or that food must always be involved in welcome. All of us can expand our limited sight to understand hospitality as something to carry wherever we go and regardless of what we have to offer.

Mirror three: Only me.
Western culture has long privatized and individualized spiritual practices and services. We often think, *How can I be hospitable?* Of course, this is not the wrong question to ask, but it is not the only question we should ask. Hospitality is best practiced in the community, alongside others who value it. It is a posture to hold together, not alone.

Author and professor Christine Pohl says of the early church communities that they worked together to provide space for others: "There was never an assumption that individual households alone could care for large numbers of needy strangers."

These early church communities never assumed that one household could care for others all by itself. We so readily assume that problems are to be solved by individuals, rather than by a robust community of both strangers and friends working together.

Each year, our neighborhood high school has a march-a-thon. During this march-a-thon, the marching band goes up and down the streets, playing a few of its competition and rallying songs. If you donate significantly to the band, they will stop at your home and play a few songs. My family has paid this significant donation over the last few years, and it has led to far more people congregating on our front lawn than could ever walk into our house. Now, if you told us that we had to host over a hundred people inside our home, all on our own, we would be overwhelmed. We'd say, "No way." But we don't have to do it this way. Instead, we put out coffee and a few breakfast items on our front lawn and ask our neighbors to share their yards. The parents of kids in the band are delighted to come over and help host. By extending hospitality outside our home to multiple yards, and with the help of other community members to host, we can host an event for all.

We can become people of welcome who then invite others to join us in being people of welcome: friends, neighborhood, church community, and beyond. The strength of hospitality increases in community. We're not meant to be hospitable on our own.

Mirror four: Interruptions.

A final mirror to our understanding of hospitality: interruptions. Interruptions give us a quick glimpse of our posture. They have a way of getting under our skin, but can help our posture if we choose to let them. This mirror is not new to our time or culture.

Jesus often used stories to interrupt us, revealing the posture of our heart toward the stranger.

In the Gospel of Luke, a lawyer asks Jesus honest questions about eternal life. Jesus responds with his own questions, helping the lawyer to consider what it means to love one's neighbor. The lawyer thinks eternal life is about checking off the boxes of being good and Jesus shares with him a story about love that permits interruption, requires mercy, and stops and cares for the stranger. It's a story of mercy, in which the merciful one cares for his neighbor until he is fully restored (Luke 10:25-37). It is just like Jesus to break down our boxes.

Court Appointed Special Advocates (CASA) volunteers advocate for children who have experienced abuse and neglect with the hope of helping them into safe and protected homes. They come to mind when I think of those who have expanded their box of hospitality to include heart, compassion, and care. These men and women allow themselves to be affected by our youngest neighbors. They advocate in unjust systems, care for those who have been abandoned, and spill their own tears with the heartbreak of those who suffer. When we allow Jesus to break down the walls of our box of hospitality, we welcome the vulnerable and open ourselves up to the stories of those we care for. It is not only our schedule that hospitality interrupts, but our hearts and agendas as well. We often want to keep the box closed and clean, a mere checkmark to be completed without any personal cost. Having a limited understanding of hospitality is far easier and more comfortable. It keeps us safe and unaffected. But such a perspective not only denies joy and hope for others; it also diminishes our own experience of life.

Self-reflection with a mirror can be uncomfortable and even painful. Yet looking in a mirror can be an incredible gift. The mirrors mentioned above give us the opportunity to be honest, bring our self-knowledge to Jesus, and work with others toward a posture of hospitality. Welcome can be so much more than we have imagined. Pay attention to what you find through self-reflection, and allow these mirrors to open up the possibility of what might be. And Jesus is the master of possibility. When Jesus expands our definition of hospitality, he deepens who we are and extends who we see. In this way he takes hospitality and multiplies it through us taking greater joy, love, and grace into our worlds. This moment when the deepening begins is the hardest and requires honest questions and curious exploration. And it is worth it. Your heart and the hearts of others are well worth it.

GOD STOPS AND SEES

The story of Jesus and a desperate and discarded woman illustrates the depth and extension of hospitality. Jesus was on his way to heal a desperately ill child, and a woman interrupted him along the way. She longed for healing, but had had her hope dashed for twelve years. She didn't want to bother Jesus; maybe she felt like she had been a bother to everyone else for the past twelve years. She reached out for what she needed, and didn't ask for anything. Yet Jesus paused his schedule and lavished healing on her in more ways than one (Mark 5:25-34). After restoring her physically, he restored her socially to make her faith public before the crowd. Her act of reaching out made her vulnerable. In calling her to speak, Jesus invited her to greater vulnerability—and then he gave her more than she could have imagined.

Jesus gives us so much when we include him and serve with him. And then he empowers us to offer so much to those around us. Hospitality provides and restores far more than what a person can see. When we see and extend hospitality to those around us, wherever we are, we extend God's love and mercy beyond the boxes and buildings. We are restoring a part of their humanity that may have been broken. We offer healing to their inner wounds of invisibility when they have long felt unseen. We extend love and dignity as we listen to their story and hear their faith. As we see the unseen parts and help make them whole, we meet them practically in care and love. When we hold the posture of hospitality, we provide and make space for a restoration that is even more than we can imagine. Let's dive in.

THE SHAPE OF THIS BOOK

At the end of each chapter, you will find a spiritual practice that will strengthen your posture of hospitality. The practices are varied in length and type, inviting you to grow more deeply in your relationship with God, knowledge of yourself, and service to others. As you finish each chapter, spend some time engaging with the spiritual practices. Slow down and allow space for self-reflection, interaction with God, and the Holy Spirit to transform you.

In addition to the spiritual practices at the end of each chapter, there is a group discussion guide at the end of the book. This is a helpful tool to create conversation with a small group, a staff team, or friends and family.

The Spiritual Practice of Reflection and Redefinition

Much as I guided my directee Lori, I'd love to guide you in a practice of reflection and redefinition. We will use this practice as a mirror to reflect and redefine our definition of hospitality in order to align our posture to the heart of God.

The following reflection questions will take you on a journey of remembering so that you can arrive at a redefinition of hospitality. From this redefinition, you can practice taking hospitality wherever you are. We will explore our contexts soon; for now, we will look toward the transformation of our minds and hearts to transform our posture.

As we begin, I ask for one thing: be honest as you look in the mirror, for it will lead to freedom.

Start with this base definition of *hospitality*: "Hospitality is a posture of welcome we take wherever we go."

* Set aside twenty to thirty minutes in a quiet, uninter-rupted space for this reflection and redefinition time. Allow these questions to guide you through your current image of hospitality.
* Before diving in, take a few minutes to be silent and allow your heart, mind, and body to settle a bit.
* As you settle in, think back to a time you felt welcomed, loved, and cared for—a time when you were most free to be you, without fear of consequences or judgment. This may have been a time of great need, fun celebration, or maybe even both. Think back to this time and imagine being there again. Take as long as you need to get back into that head and heart space.

* As you keep your heart and mind in that place, look around you at what is happening. Take in the environment again and the people you are with. Who is there, and what are they doing? What is the atmosphere like? Does it feel or look a certain way? What is being provided for you?

* Write down the environment, the people, and the moment you felt most free and seen. Perhaps this moment was short, or it may have extended many minutes.

* As you reflect on this moment, what were you being given? How did it feel? What was it like? Write this down.

* Now consider what it took or what it cost for that person or those people to extend this gift to you. What does this tell you about who they are? Use adjectives to describe their actions and write them down.

* Take these adjectives from the answered questions at that moment and fill in the blanks with your own words.

* When I was extended hospitality, I felt _____, _____, and _____.

* Those who extended hospitality were _____, _____, and _____.

* Now, take these adjectives and include them in our understanding that hospitality is a posture of welcome we take wherever we go. Use this example if helpful:

> To have a posture of hospitality is to extend _____, _____, and _____ to another.

* Sit with this definition with God in prayer. Hold onto it as we move into our next chapter of considering our contexts.

2

THE PLACES YOU ARE

WEARING A ROBE IS FOR graduations or luxury hotels—or so I thought. Yet I found myself wearing a robe for my profession as a pastor. God had given me a curveball in my vocation, which led to me staring in a bathroom mirror, in a full black robe, about to lead worship from a chancel (that's the stage in some churches). I had thought I was going to be an overseas missionary. But here I was in a local church bathroom, wearing a tailored robe, getting ready to lead a worship service.

"What am I doing?" I asked.

And I sensed God say, "Would you wear the clothes of the people overseas and not wear the clothes of the people here?"

So I stepped into a new context, in an unexpected vocation, to love a people.

UNEXPECTED CONTEXTS

Many of us can name contexts in which we didn't expect ourselves to be: a city or job, a stage of marriage or singleness, a social status, or a school. We find ourselves in unexpected contexts and circumstances. Getting there might have been our doing or someone else's. God may have guided us in some way.

No matter how we get to these places, we can have a purpose within unexpected contexts.

When I think about this topic, I consider the often-taken-out-of-context verse from Jeremiah: "'For I know the plans I have for you,' declares the LORD, 'plans to prosper you and not to harm you, plans to give you hope and a future'" (Jeremiah 29:11).

Let's talk about the historical background for a minute. This prophecy comes during the Israelites' seventy-year exile, in which God has brought his chosen people from their home of Jerusalem to the far-off city of Babylon. The Israelites are now foreigners in a foreign land. A place of different values, language, and culture. *God* brought them here. And in his words through the prophet Jeremiah, he doesn't promise it will only be a few years. He tells them to root themselves, plant gardens, build houses, grow their families, and to remain. He tells them to seek peace, prosperity, and blessing for this city. God then says that he will return after seventy years and bring his people back home. At this point, we hear the verse quoted above. Jeremiah 29:11 is given to the Israelites while they are in a context they do not want. They are told to stay and flourish, to bless those around them, and trust God.

I can imagine that this is not what the Israelites wanted to hear! I imagine they wanted to go home; I imagine that they wanted the blessing of Jeremiah 29:11 for their homeland, with the language, culture, and freedoms they knew. But God called the Israelites to do good, hard, and worthy work. And he promised to see and remember this work.

Ask anyone who knows me and they know I grumble about the city I live in. When I moved here for seminary, I told God that I would stay for two to three years, at most. Here I am over twenty years later in a concrete city that would dry out even the soul of

Jesus (just kidding, but you know what I mean). And twenty years later I still long to live in the mountains, to listen to a babbling brook, and to live in the grandeur of creation. Comparatively, my city is no Babylon, yet living here has been hard on my soul. In God's grace, what I have received is a beautiful church community, an extended family where cousins, aunts, and uncles live just miles apart, and the gift of a God who nourishes my soul in a parched land.

Contexts can be hard. They can be dry. Still, God is there.

WORKING OUR CONTEXTS

In addition to a robe, in my new church vocation, I had to learn a new language with words like *chancel, narthex,* and *moderator.* Never mind the unfamiliar acronyms that included words I also didn't know. Gratefully, my third-culture-kid upbringing taught me how to read context clues, so my brain went to work interpreting this new place and calling. I had to humbly surrender to the ways and manners of the culture to enter that place with purpose.

The work of hospitality lies in learning the contexts we have been called to, seeing beyond what is obvious, and living our purpose in those places to bring good. And the contexts we are called to are numerous. We walk into local stores, schools, and neighborhoods. We dwell in places for the long term or the short term. Sometimes we carry hospitality to familiar spaces and faces; sometimes, we need to carry it to surprises and sudden situations. Developing the muscles of learning contexts helps us see how God calls us into both familiar and foreign places.

Taking ten minutes to look over your calendar will reveal the familiar places you go. The grocery store, the office, a coffee shop, a school, your walking path, the gym, the church building. There are regular places you show up and know what to expect. Maybe you engage with familiar faces and people and avoid others—as we all do. Maybe you decide to linger in a conversation at the coffee shop, but you don't pause when you're at the gym. Different factors drive your various responses. Hospitality in one place looks different from hospitality in another. Hospitality to one person looks different from hospitality to another.

Maybe you take a regular walk. One day, you have limited time to get back home for an event for your child. On another day, you don't have anything on the calendar after your walk, so you have more time. Is being present for your child any more or less hospitable than stopping to talk to your widowed neighbor? Hospitality on one day can look different on another day. And these decisions are not mutually exclusive. Our hospitality can vary depending on our context, our time, and those around us.

To allow hospitality to move into known and unknown contexts, we need to expand our definition to include the posture we hold rather than a given time, space, and formula. Let's consider the limits we start with.

Some limiting formulas might include:

* A lot of time + food = hospitality
* A beautiful space + saying hello to everyone = hospitality
* Clean house + meeting needs = hospitality
* What would your formula be? _____ + _____ = hospitality

These formulas are not incorrect, but they are limiting.

Mine did not include robes and words like *chancel* and *narthex*, but God's definition sure did.

When we limit when, where, and how hospitality can happen, we limit the power of authentic connection and moments of deepening and strengthened faith. Wherever we are, we can carry hospitality so that others might see and experience the rich love that the God of the universe has for them. It's a love that meets them where they are and cares deeply for them. A warmth that welcomes them.

GENUINE PRESENCE

Jesus also found himself a stranger and in a strange context. He created the earth, but he had never inhabited it in human form. He came at the mercy of those who would extend hospitality to him—much like the Israelites and like you and me when we find ourselves in foreign contexts. As John says,

> The true light, which gives light to everyone, was coming into the world. He was in the world, and the world was made through him, yet the world did not know him. He came to his own, and his own people did not receive him. But to all who did receive him, who believed in his name, he gave the right to become children of God. (John 1:9-12 ESV)

Even as Jesus had power, he chose genuine presence and dwelling. Theologian Amy Oden says,

> Hospitality does not entail helping another so much as immersing oneself in a new reality, entering into a new relationship with one who before was unknown or unappreciated. The nothing of "being with the other" values presence more than outcome. The success of hospitality, however, does not depend on end results. Rather, the success of hospitality is measured by the degree to which one offers one's genuine

presence with another, to fully enter another's world and dwell with another.

Before Jesus' arrival on earth, God dwelled closely with people in many different ways, like a pillar of fire and a cloud at night. God showed up in a burning bush and a whisper. And, of course, he showed up with literal human skin and lived with us. When we do the work of hospitality in our contexts, we can bring love and welcome through our genuine presence.

Some dear friends of mine worked in a major city with a ministry that took the gospel to the streets. Their goal was to bring the love of Jesus to the unhoused. Did they meet, shelter, and feed people experiencing houselessness? Absolutely. However, their primary purpose was to meet these people where they were with the love of Jesus—on the streets, in their context.

The city government got involved and became a partner of this ministry. To get people experiencing houselessness off the streets, the city began to buy apartment buildings and old hotels so that people experiencing houselessness could be moved from the streets to private rooms. This provision benefits the image of the city. However, this does not benefit the unhoused, whose community is on the streets. The city's actions compromise the mission of the organization and endanger the community of the unhoused. Hospitality is not about fixing the problems of the powerful; rather, hospitality sees the values of the community, listens to their needs, and creates spaces for others. The unhoused know their context. My friends are listening.

LEAVING OUR COMFORTS

Hospitality often means leaving our comforts. It is clear that Jesus did so. And often, we can choose to be like him. The challenge is that many of us are comfortable in our contexts. This statement is not a judgment; it is simply a reality. We know our contexts; we are familiar with the people, the places, and the social graces. We may well have seen God at work in beautiful ways in these good and comfortable places. Yet there are times that God calls us to venture out into new spaces. This may not necessarily mean a cross-country move, but it may entail a cross-the-street walk. We may be called to people we don't know in places we don't know—maybe even languages and social cues we don't know. It takes courage to carry hospitality and the stories of God's faithfulness to these new places.

Sometimes, returning home *is* leaving comfort. We sometimes return to familiar contexts as different people. This return home is a unique challenge: we have changed and we are reentering a context that knew us as different people before. We are susceptible to returning back to our ways before rather than bringing new goodness and care with us.

Luke 8 tells the story of a healed man who longs to go with Jesus rather than return home. Instead, "Jesus sent him away, saying, 'Return home and tell how much God has done for you.' So the man went away and told all over town how much Jesus had done for him" (Luke 8:38-39).

Sometimes Jesus calls us to return home. The truth is that returning home is challenging for many of us, including myself. I've shared the joys and gifts of my family, but it is still like every other family: imperfect. I love adventures and new people and places. Returning home is not how I'm wired. Yet returning home is sometimes needed. We return to care for a loved one. We return for a particular relationship. We return for the sake of others. Sometimes, we return to a place we do not prefer. And often, this return is a step of faith.

We don't know the exact circumstances of the demon-possessed man, but we can imagine his longing to stay with the one who made him whole. Surely this would be more appealing than returning to a place where he was known only in sickness. It took courage to return, and he did so, bringing with him a story of Jesus' healing and restoration.

Whatever context we walk into, we take stories of God's hospitality, healing, and restoration. We share stories of hopefulness and provide a picture of what might be possible in another's life. What stories of God's faithfulness, healing, and restoration do you carry with you?

The Spiritual Practice of Listening

As you have considered some of your contexts, one practice that will strengthen your hospitality and welcome is the spiritual practice of listening—both listening to God and listening to others.

Before we can listen well to others, we must begin with listening to God. We need to listen for what God is saying to us and for us, and what God is calling us to.

Listening to God

* Make a list of your known contexts.
* Write down what you believe about these contexts, including:

    - Assumptions
    - Information
    - Expectations
    - Responsibilities

* Spend some time praying over your responses, asking God to show you anything he wants to highlight for you to pay attention to.
* Using the same known contexts, respond to the questions:

    - What do I need to be curious about?
    - What is mine to do?
    - Is there an outcome I need to let go of?

* Again, spend time praying over your responses, asking God to make known to you things he is calling you to surrender, the ways he is calling you to humility, and the responsibilities that are yours to carry.

Listening to Others

Continuing our practice of listening, consider listening through the illustration of being an illuminator. In an article called "The

Essential Skills for Being Human," NY Times opinion columnist David Brooks discusses *illuminators* and *diminishers*. Diminishers make quick assumptions based on one piece of evidence about you; illuminators remain curious and make others feel "bigger, respected, and lit up."

He then gives the following illustration of an illuminator:

Many years ago, patent lawyers at Bell Labs were trying to figure out why some employees were much more productive than others. They explored almost every possible explanation—educational background, position in the company—and came up empty. Then they noticed a quirk. Many of the most productive researchers were in the habit of having breakfast or lunch with an electrical engineer named Harry Nyquist. Nyquist really listened to their challenges, got inside their heads, brought out the best in them.

Brooks goes on to say:

The illuminators offer the privilege of witness. They take the anecdotes, rationalizations, and episodes we tell and see us in a noble struggle. They see the way we're navigating the dialectics of life—intimacy versus independence, control versus freedom—and understand that our current selves are just where we are right now on our long continuum of growth.

As listeners, we can witness the life of another, allowing them to be human, joining in with our attention, accompaniment, conversation, and care.

How can we serve as illuminators and listen to those in our contexts?

We slow down, make space, and hold stories.

We slow down.

The first movement toward hospitality is slowing down. We must slow down to notice those around us and see another person as a human being rather than someone to use, get past, or just ignore. We must slow down our speech and our immediate responses to people, giving them time to expand or extend their thoughts, feelings, and words. Slowing down is the first step.

We make space.

As we slow down, we must also make space, particularly *negative space*. In art, negative space is space that helps to clarify, simplify, and give focus. Consider one practical space: our calendar. If we want to be illuminators, what we think must be done must decrease. This is simple and practical. We need negative space in which we aren't moving toward a goal or manifesting potential. These rest times restore and create space in our hearts and minds that, in turn, illumine the rest of our days.

What needs to be taken off your calendar?

We hold stories.

Eugene Peterson wrote, "Stories open doors to areas or aspects of life that we didn't know were there, or had quit noticing out of over-familiarity, or supposed were out-of-bounds. They then welcome us in. Stories are verbal acts of hospitality." We hold stories of God's faithfulness as we bring them to mind, read Scripture, and listen to them. We hold our stories by slowing down and noticing the movement of God in our lives. And we hold the stories of others as we listen. We give them space to share their thoughts, their experiences, their hopes, and their pains.

In hospitality, we hold each other's stories and see a God that meets us in faithfulness and love. In our humanity, we humble ourselves to meet someone where they are. When we listen, we are able to love.

THE FIRST HOST

3

WHEN MY PARENTS IMMIGRATED to the United States, they were at the mercy of those who would receive them. My dad came to the United States first, with friends, to figure out the lay of the land. They scouted two cities where they knew people and began to settle. My mom and brother followed, joining him in this new place of opportunity.

This meant, among other things, opportunities to learn. English would become their third language. America's landscape, terrain, and people would be quite different from where they came from. They had investigated the country carefully, but they both had to enter with vulnerability and trust. They made their move based on their hope for a better life and the good stories of those who had experienced the United States before them. Vulnerability and trust are always at play when we are guests, since we do not have the power to control our environment.

Guests are at the mercy of the hosts, who hold power. Maybe that is why most of us would rather be hosts than guests. But if we want to cultivate hospitality, we need the regular work of being guests. When we host, we often assume that we can begin with power, privilege, and possibility. This posture is not always wrong, but regularly assuming this role leads us to forget that we are more often the guests—the less powerful ones. Our hospitality cannot begin with us, with what we can provide, or even our privileges, but with what has been given to us. The posture of a host requires humility, and one of the best ways is to remember that all has been given to us and to remember it with gratitude. Every good gift has been given to us by God, and rests in the initiative of the first and greatest host: God (James 1:17). As we recognize and receive God as our first and greatest host, we extend the gifts we have been given freely to others.

SINCE THE BEGINNING

Humanity has been hosted from the beginning of time. The land, waters, sea, and sky welcomed the first man and woman. "In the beginning God created the heavens and the earth. Now the earth was formless and empty, darkness was over the surface of the deep, and the Spirit of God was hovering over the waters" (Genesis 1:1-2). Returning to these beginnings, we are invited to remember and see anew the hospitality of the triune God.

God's presence, words, and action put our world into existence. The story of creation from above continues in the expanse of the earth, skies, and space, describing the separation of light and dark, morning and night, earth and sky, land and sea, seed-bearing plants and trees, sun and moon, sea animals and flying birds, and animals to roam the land (Genesis 1:3-25). No one can fathom all the pieces of matter, solids, liquids, and gases, as well as other seen and unseen materials, that God designs and gives place. After all this space-making and movement, God creates humankind in God's likeness (Genesis 1:26-27) and gives everything to them (Genesis 1:28-29). God establishes, creates, orders, and provides the first home for humankind. God is the ultimate first host, and humanity, made in God's image, will also be a host in this world.

Theologian Amy Oden, who has studied and written extensively on hospitality, says,

> The larger spiritual context in which hospitality is practiced always begins with God. These early texts draw the reader's attention first to what God is doing and only secondarily to what oneself or one's community is doing. God offers hospitality to all humanity, first by establishing a home (*oikos*) for all. Second, God offers an abundant grace that pulls us into God's presence and life. Through God's hospitality we can participant in the divine life and be saved therein.

Whenever we read of good in the world, that good began with God. Whenever we experience love from another, that love began with God. Our ability to love, provide good, and host comes from the first host.

In hosting, God provides a home, grace, presence, life, and participation in that life. He provides a space for all our needs, generosity through his gracious being with us, life itself through his breath, and purpose and participation in life. The elements of hospitality are found in God before they are found in any human being. God imparts each of these elements to us so that we might provide home, grace, presence, life, participation, and purpose to others.

HOSTED ON THE JOURNEY

The Camino de Santiago in Spain hosts hundreds of thousands of spiritual journeyers each year, referred to as *peregrinos* or pilgrims. 2023 was the year the Camino hosted me. It was my first time combining extensive walking with the spiritual practices. Most of the leaders that were hosting were strangers to me, but because I was familiar with the organization, I trusted them. Each morning, we walked in solitude and silence, interacting with God as we put one foot in front of the other. We were told not to break our silence until noon so that we could be attentive to God's voice in our lives. Each morning, I would pause before going downstairs to breakfast and allow God to give me a word that I would hold as a theme for the day.

On the third day of walking, God gave me the word "music" as the theme for the day. I was emotionally tender as I started the day as my daughter had been struggling back home. In the morning, God invited me to go slowly and be gentle with my pace, a contrast to the previous days when I had felt in charge of my pace and day. I welcomed the tender invitation to go as gently as the Spirit's pace allowed. Along with these invitations was the invitation to include music in my day, so I decided I would listen to my daughter's favorite music in the afternoon to stay connected and close to her. Little did I know that this was an invitation to welcome the music God would provide.

Before our walk, our teammate and chapel leader led us in a song. The song was the exact song my daughter and I would regularly sing when she was a little girl. In fact, the only video we have of us singing is of this song. In that moment, I realized God was providing the music. He invited and provided before I could jump in to take care of it. It was such a sweet moment of being held and seen by God, knowing he was going before me and with me and would provide the way.

Then God offered another moment of music. As we walked silently through a forest, the sound of a babbling brook and bagpipes filled the air. A babbling brook is where my soul is immediately at rest and open to God. And the bagpipes were, again, God's music of choice for me. Bagpipes are the typical instrument for memorial services in my Presbyterian church. And as I sat by the babbling brook with the bagpipes nearby, I heard God invite me to consider anything that I was carrying that was already dead and to let it go. The music of funerals invited me to let go and freed my soul. Again, God knew what I needed and provided it. He knew I needed to be held in deeper ways than I knew.

Now, in everyday life, as I hear God's invitations and remember God going before me, I more readily look to see what God has already provided. I still try to take care of things, but every once in a while, I consider pausing and looking to see if God has already provided. When God gives me an invitation, maybe it is for me to see what he might do rather than go ahead and take over. Maybe when God gives an invitation, I should allow him to be the host and trust him as his guest.

STRUGGLE TO RECEIVE

Even as God goes before us with good gifts, we often struggle to remain guests and to receive. We think: *I must take care of this, because no one else will.* We take it upon ourselves to make sure things happen. Then, we question whether we have done enough and if God is satisfied. But God never asked us to satisfy him. God is the one who promises to satisfy us.

Our longing to be safe is so strong that we look for all the ways to grasp the power that we think will protect us. So we take over. This manifests itself in our hospitality: as hosts, we are able to change, control, invite, exclude, and manage what is happening.

As hosts, we can ensure things are safe for ourselves even while we look to serve others.

So often, we want the comfort of being hosts. After all, being the host comes with a sense of control and power. But God regularly calls us to lay down our ways and trust his ways. Sometimes, we think of our controlling tendencies as indicating responsibility or good stewardship—but if we are honest with ourselves, control is usually about our sense of safety and comfort. We prefer managing our gifts rather than trusting the One who has given us everything.

Yet, even God, the first and greatest host, the One with all power, authority, and control, chose to become a guest. Even as God is the first and greatest host, he chose to become vulnerable, move out of his predictable environment, give up power, open himself up to the pain and sufferings of this world, and live among his creation. His love is so expansive that he became vulnerable and lived in solidarity with us.

Jesus' vulnerability made way for an even greater gift: salvation.

Vulnerability. Surrender. Sacrifice. Salvation.

Big words. Big God.

When we remain the host, we are unable to receive the gifts that God has for us and extend greater gifts to others. When we choose to remain in power, we are safe but not seen. We are sheltered, but we cannot receive God's goodness and grace. We can give to others only from our limited resources, while God wants to lavish us and others with his infinite love. Faithful and promise-filled love is the kind of love he invites us into. Yet we would rather play it safe with power, because sometimes love is too vulnerable.

The following assessment can help us recognize how we receive hospitality. Go ahead and take a minute to respond to the questions.

On a scale of 1-10, with 10 being the highest:

* ✳ How would you rate your welcome of God?
* ✳ How would you rate your welcome of yourself?
* ✳ How would you rate your welcome of others?
* ✳ What do you make of your results?

When I administer this assessment, I hear a typical pattern of responses. People rate their welcome of others highest, and they rate their welcome of themselves the lowest. Their welcome of God tends to fall in the middle range.

Most people report that they assume a hospitable posture. Having a hospitable posture is a good thing! Yet the mid-level score for our welcome of God illustrates that many of us have a theological understanding that hospitality comes from us. Many of us have heard in churches, schools, and homes that we must continually give more than we have received. Often we assume we must muster up welcome when we do not know welcome for ourselves. This theology assumes that we have a power that we don't have—so no matter what, the responsibility for hospitality is up to us.

God generously invites us to continue to know God's welcome. When we say, "No, thanks, I've got it," we trust and rely on our capacity rather than God's. And it is God's capacity that is endless. Receiving requires vulnerability and trust, and the God who first invites is the One who will also provide. We are invited to trust the landscape he created for us, and to trust that he is with us. We are invited to trust that he knows what we need before we know it. And fortunately, he persistently and consistently reminds us of these truths.

WELCOMING OUR LONGINGS

Armenian culture has a sneaky back-and-forth dynamic—and unless you know about it, you won't recognize it. (This is the case with most cultural phenomena, of course, and not uniquely Armenian.) Here is the sneakiness: we never accept the first invitation offered. Ever. There is always a back-and-forth between an invitation and a decline. Always. There's a rhythm: the host says "come," and the guest says "no, thank you." Then another "come" and "no, no," and then one final "come" and, at last, an "okay." These three cycles of invitation and decline are what we do. We never say yes to the first invitation. In fact, it is shameful to say yes the first time.

I remember being struck when my American friends would say yes immediately to a snack offered. In contrast, even when I wanted a snack, I would say no the first time. When I declined, the hosts never offered again, and I went without my snack because I couldn't follow up with a yes without a new invitation. The cultural miscue led to wrong assumptions, either that Americans weren't hospitable (incorrect) or that Armenians didn't want snacks (also incorrect). Fortunately, I have learned a bit about our cultures now. I either say yes the first time, or I fight my shame and come back to ask for a snack after declining—because I love snacks.

Knowing Jesus' Jewishness, and his home context of the Middle East, warms my heart, because I see him welcoming us persistently. Jesus doesn't stop saying, "Come and receive." He doesn't refrain from inviting us to pause and be nourished. He regularly invites us to stay awhile. And the beauty is that saying no to his first offer doesn't mean we cannot say yes to his second or third. Even if we say no, we need not be ashamed to come back and say, "Actually, I do want that."

Much deeper than our longing for a snack is our longing to be welcomed, seen, and loved. And we are often unaware of it. Sometimes, this longing is buried deep within, and we cannot see or know it, yet God does. That, I think, is why he repeats himself. He knows our deepest longings and wants to meet them, so he repeatedly says, "Come." And we have more and more opportunities to say yes even after many denials. God's welcome appeals to the deepest parts of ourselves. His hospitality waits for us with love, goodness, and grace. We can say yes at any time.

SEEING GOD'S HOSPITALITY

A few years ago, I had the opportunity to lead a retreat in Florida. As I walked on the sidewalk next to the shoreline, I noticed the plants, flowers, and the gardener who gently cared for them. As I did so, I thanked God that I could behold such beauty. My job was to host the retreat, and I saw myself hosting the earth's beauty and the gardeners tending to it. But in a split second, I sensed the Holy Spirit adjust my view and say, "Actually, creation is holding you." My immediate response was, "What?" But again, the Spirit reminded me, "Creation is holding you. This earth you walk on, this solid ground, the beauty around you, is holding you."

In that moment, I was reminded of the great care of God's hands. The same hands that had the power to move the deep darkness and separate the land and the sea in the very beginning also held me. Through his creation, he held me. Through the invitation of the Spirit, he held me. I needed to be reminded that I was held. New beauty, peace, and joy entered my heart and mind, and my grip on hosting loosened. My hands could open to receive what might come. Even as I was nourishing others, he was nourishing me.

We all need regular reminders of God's love, grace, and power holding us. These reminders readjust us to being receivers of the great gifts God has for us that we might offer them to others. Christine Pohl says, "Hospitality is at the heart of the Christian life, drawing from God's grace and reflecting God's graciousness. In hospitality, we respond to the welcome that God has offered and replicate that welcome in the world."

We are called to do what God does. We were created in his image, and this includes being hosts. Just as Jesus does everything he sees the Father doing, we do everything God does. How can we know what he does if we don't regularly receive it?

The Spiritual Practice of Receiving and Replicating

If our welcome draws from God's welcome, then we must receive in order to replicate. Often this happens on a cyclical, rather than linear, timeline. As we grow in receiving God's love, accepting his power, and trusting him, we are able to give more of God's love, use our power for good, and build welcome and trust with our fellow human beings.

There are so many ways to practice receiving God's love. One way is through reflecting on the love we have received from God as Father and Mother, God the Son, and God the Spirit. Even as they are all one, each has provided for us in different ways. Spend some time considering what you have received from each through the following prompts. After this, you will be asked how you might replicate the triune God in the places and spaces you are called to.

Receiving

Triune God the Creator. The triune God spoke and moved the world into existence.

* How have you received places of beauty and creation in your life?

As you reflect on these spaces, imagine how they have held your heart, mind, body, and soul. Express thanks to God for creation.

God the Father and Mother. God our Father and Mother has provided the context of family for us. The language of family is used throughout Scripture and extends beyond our biological families, though it does include those.

* How have you been welcomed into family in your life?

As you reflect on these places and people, express thanks to God for each person and place.

God the Son. In Jesus, God became flesh and lived on the earth. He walked and talked among us and experienced the myriad of human emotions from joy to anger, delight to sorrow. He chose to enter as we are in the world.

* How have you received Jesus' solidarity of humanity in your life, including in your joy, anger, delight, and sorrow?

As you reflect on this solidarity with Jesus, allow it to sink deeper into your heart, mind, body, and soul.

God the Spirit. In the Holy Spirit, we have the promise of always having a home in God. Jesus left us with the Spirit, who is with us always to encourage, strengthen, guide, and advocate for us.

* How has the promise of the Spirit reminded you that you always have a home in God, and he has never and will never leave you?
* How might you practice remembering?

Replicating

As followers of Jesus, having our home in the triune God, we replicate the ways of welcome that God has provided in our world. This replication is rooted in our receiving.

* In the ways that you receive, how can you now replicate God's welcome in the places and spaces you go?

Creating. God's presence, words, and movement in the earth were a part of creation.

* As a cocreator, how can you replicate presence to those around you?
* How might your words create welcome for another?
* How might you move things around in order to provide places of welcome, including actions that lead to justice and service to others?
* Where is there beauty you can create?

Spend some time imagining whether presence, words, or movement can be a way you can replicate God's welcome in the places and spaces you go.

Family. God regularly extended and extends family beyond biology. As the perfect Father and Mother, God provides good gifts and extends these good gifts to others.

* How might you extend family to those who don't have this type of good family surrounding them?

Solidarity. The great gift of Jesus is salvation, and that was made possible first by his incarnation—his choice to be with us. We cannot save others, but we can choose to be with them in their greatest joys and deepest griefs.

* Who in your life needs this solidarity? How could you sit with them, listen to them, and join their world?

Staying with. The Spirit is always with us. We will never be left by God. We can give this gift of staying to others; it is a gift that our lonely world needs, to know they will not be abandoned.

* Who are the people that you need to stay with? How can you, in doing so, replicate God's committed presence with us?

4

COUNTERFEIT HOSPITALITY

EVERY DAY, MY FAMILY WALKED between Persian Armenian and American cultures. Armenian, English, and Farsi were all spoken in our home, and it was common for all three languages to be intertwined in a single sentence. Basmati rice and pita bread were our standard side dishes. Communication via debate and interruption filled every conversation; expressing anger was acceptable. We always chose work over play. But every time we stepped out of our home, we entered another world: one with a singular language, fast-food meals, pauses and silence in communication, hidden emotions, and regular leisure. Each day, we saw quite a contrast of worlds.

The ongoing movement between two cultures created in my family the ability to adapt to people, places, and situations. We could weave through various systems, spaces, and conversations. This ability was, and is, a great gift. Yet, as I entered different spaces, I wondered what part of myself could show up. The darker side of this weaving and adapting was that I struggled to know where I belonged. Adapting gave me agility and the ability to fit in. Yet fitting in is not belonging.

In *The Gifts of Imperfection*, social scientist Brené Brown distinguishes between belonging and fitting in: "Fitting in is about assessing a situation and becoming who you need to be to be accepted. Belonging, on the other hand, doesn't require us to change who we are; it requires us to be who we are."

The desire to fit in was so strong that I sacrificed parts of myself. I needed to survive in a new culture and among new people, so I adapted. But in fitting in, I didn't belong—because it wasn't me showing up. It took me a while to learn that I could show up, and to learn what places of true hospitality were like. Places of true hospitality not only allow us, but require us, to be ourselves. In these places, guests can offer gifts and contributions without being told to hold back or expected to stay in their lane. In these places, we are expected to show up rather than morph into what is acceptable to fit into a system or community.

To be hospitable, an environment needs to be low on fear, insecurity, and anxiety, and high on dependence, curiosity, gratitude, and belonging. Any space with high levels of fear, insecurity, and stress will demand fitting in rather than belonging. A culture of fear leads to judgment and cutting others off. A people of insecurity will see anyone's gifts as a threat. An environment of anxiety wants to keep things in order and the same.

Too many places are beset by fear, insecurity, and anxiety. These spaces welcome, but with limits: come, but you have to look and speak and contribute in certain ways. In these places, participating consists of toeing the party line and fitting in, not cultivating a space where people belong and are nourished. This is counterfeit hospitality. Sadly, we can't always see and feel that it is counterfeit. Too often, we accept it as the real thing.

FROM HOSPITALITY TO HOSTILITY

The places that welcome us with counterfeit hospitality can seem like the real thing at first. At first we feel warmth, welcome, and excitement. We become a part of the culture and people, and make deep friendships. But then we take a slight step out of line and the warmth turns cold. We begin to receive hostility rather than hospitality.

When Jesus returned to his hometown to teach and minister to the people there, he faced such an environment. A place where he was once welcomed quickly turned to a place of hostility. His disciples watched as he was ridiculed and rejected. In this environment, he taught his disciples how to discern and see the real thing. It wouldn't be the last time this would happen.

> Jesus left there and went to his hometown, accompanied by his disciples. When the Sabbath came, he began to teach in the synagogue, and many who heard him were amazed.
>
> "Where did this man get these things?" they asked. "What's this wisdom that has been given him? What are these remarkable miracles he is performing? Isn't this the carpenter? Isn't this Mary's son and the brother of James, Joseph, Judas and Simon? Aren't his sisters here with us?" And they took offense at him.
>
> Jesus said to them, "A prophet is not without honor except in his own town, among his relatives and in his own home." He could not do any miracles there, except lay his hands on a few sick people and heal them. He was amazed at their lack of faith.
>
> Then Jesus went around teaching from village to village. (Mark 6:1-6)

Jesus returns to his hometown and begins teaching and healing. The townspeople's curiosity about what he is doing quickly turns to criticism about who Jesus is. They move from wondering where he received his teaching, wisdom, and miraculous abilities to criticizing his character and his parentage. Their hospitality turns to hostility, and as a result, Jesus is only able to heal a few sick people.

Note that it was not only Jesus who suffered from this hostility. The townspeople inflicted suffering on themselves. Can you imagine those who were watching Jesus heal and hoping for their turn? They saw the life, healing, dreams, and joy his wisdom and touch would bring—and they watched their own community deny it.

Often, hospitality doesn't turn to outright hostility. Instead, it turns cold and withdraws from others—ending up in passive-aggressive and silent hostility. Many have faced this, regardless of culture, gender, or age. Counterfeit hospitality is when hospitality looks real at first but then shows its true face.

In American churches, the elderly often experience counterfeit hospitality. The church has welcomed their gifts and generosity for decades, but when they cannot do as much or require more care, their communities disregard and dismiss them. The moment they become less useful and more needy, the church withholds hospitality, because their ideas, age, and slower movement threaten the expansion of the church. When we ignore the elderly in this way, we are dishonoring them. We are missing out on the beauty and goodness they continue to bring to the community.

On the other side of the age spectrum is a phenomenon called "ghosting." This is an action when a person simply ignores another's communication in order to cut off a relationship. It can be emotionally troubling, as the relationship ends without closure. It might cause one to wonder what they did wrong or why someone left without saying goodbye. It can also cause one to wonder whether their relationship, and the welcome they experienced in it, was real. Many of us may have experienced this in our work contexts. We have been told that we are valued and welcomed, yet find ourselves overlooked for promotions, opportunities, and growth.

Whatever the context, most people have experienced this: thinking you were welcomed, and then realizing that the welcome only extended to one limited version of yourself. Maybe it was the version of you that didn't cause interruptions or changes. Perhaps it was the version of you that kept the institution or organizational machine going. As long as you fit in, you were fine. But the desire to fit in meant that people's gifts were lost. In counterfeit hospitality, everyone misses out.

WISDOM AND WELCOME

Even as there is pain from places where welcome ends, there are gifts that come from our grief and sorrow. The realities of Jesus' experience provided the soil for seeds of wisdom, and Jesus instructed his disciples according to them.

> Calling the Twelve to him, he began to send them out two by two and gave them authority over impure spirits. These were his instructions: "Take nothing for the journey except a staff—no bread, no bag, no money in your belts. Wear sandals but not an extra shirt. Whenever you enter a house, stay there until you leave that town. And if any place will not welcome you or listen to you, leave that place and shake the dust off your feet as a testimony against them." (Mark 6:7-11)

The disciples did what he said. As they preached, they healed many people (Mark 6:12-13).

The disciples had just seen Jesus set an example of being rejected. Then they heard his instructions and wisdom for what to do when they, in turn, were rejected. One might think that Jesus would tell his disciples to be prepared, pack extra, and look to take care of themselves in the hostile world. But he gave them the counterintuitive direction to make themselves particularly vulnerable. This is not what most of us would expect.

Choosing to be vulnerable, as Jesus instructed, was an act of faith for the disciples. It provided the possibility they would be hurt. Yet at the same time, entering towns with vulnerability meant they would receive clarity. Too often, we enter spaces with our protections high, seeking to make sure we don't get hurt. Yet Jesus' words seem to indicate that this is not the wisest way. His directive to stay dependent and vulnerable would have quickly given the disciples clarity around which places were truly hospitable.

I remember applying for two significant job opportunities and being rejected for both. I told a friend about my sense of discouragement, and he replied, "At least you have clarity." His words stung at the time. I didn't want clarity, but possibility. Yet he nudged me to see the possibility in rejection.

Drawing from Jesus' experience and instruction, we can practice dependence and vulnerability. In doing so, we can receive the gift of clarity. Each time we do, we cultivate greater wisdom to discern between genuine and counterfeit hospitality. Our work is to be honest—not to hide or try to fit into a place, but to see how a place will respond to our true selves.

When he was rejected in his hometown, Jesus walked away. He let go. This walking away indicted the community that rejected him, but honored the good work he was called to do in this world.

His walking away was a loss for the community, for every person that needed to be healed.

But later, Jesus would enter another hostile environment—and this time he wouldn't walk away. He went to the cross and allowed a hostile community to take his life. He did so because it was aligned with his great purpose of healing the world. And his surrender would make way for the greatest hospitality humanity could ever be offered: salvation. The beautiful result is that whether someone has been hostile or hospitable to Jesus, the gift of salvation remains open for whoever would believe and trust him. A hostile environment couldn't stop Jesus from offering his greatest gift to us. And we get to extend this gift of welcome to others. We get to live in the world in a way that others might receive and know God's love and welcome.

WHEN TO STAY

Sometimes, we don't have the option to walk away. We must stay put in counterfeit or unwelcoming places. These environments may provide income, security, and survival for a season. Or, perhaps we are required to stay for the sake of another. At times, the greater surrender is to stay—and there is great grief in this staying. We find sorrow in being rejected. We find sorrow in not being able to bring the good that God has called us to bring to this space. There is both grief for the one rejected and the community that misses out.

Jesus was kind enough to send the disciples out two by two, so that they would never be alone. They would face many foreign places, but never on their own. And by his instructions, they could discern whether to stay or move on, considering whether a place was welcoming. Whenever we discern whether a place offers true or counterfeit hospitality, the gift of wisdom and the companionship of trusted friends and family can help us decide to stay or go on.

Walking away requires wisdom and surrender. But you might need to stay, and if you do, you are not alone. Jesus stays with you, and perhaps others might, too. Look for them. Stay together. Jesus remains with you.

PEOPLE OF AUTHENTIC WELCOME

Whether we're familiar with rejection or not, we can become people of welcome. Rejection often helps us to be more aware of those who are typically not welcome. People of welcome have often experienced rejection; they can notice the stranger or outsider more easily. Knowing how it feels, they can connect and welcome others. A few postures and practices allow us to welcome strangers and to take care of those on the fringes.

First of all, we must remain dependent and vulnerable, especially on Jesus. When we do this, we remember more easily what it is to be a stranger and recognize when someone is an outsider. In this posture, we remain tender and compassionate. Most of us do not want to stay dependent and vulnerable. We work toward independence and strength. Yet, in this pursuit, we run the risk of decreasing our dependence on Jesus. We must first receive hospitality to be able to offer it. Remaining in Jesus is how we become hospitable.

We also remain in places of hospitality. We remain in places that welcome us so that we might use the good gifts God has given us. We cultivate gratitude and a deeper understanding of genuine hospitality as we remain. So often, we are looking for the next greener pasture. Staying in a place that has welcomed us develops our muscles of dependence. Given this good and healthy understanding of hospitality, we can better recognize places of counterfeit hospitality. When we choose to stay within hospitable places and express our gratitude for them, we deepen hospitality, security, and welcome of others.

To continue to be people of welcome, we remain generous, offering the gifts God has given us to those around us. Remaining in Jesus and remaining in the places of hospitality, we grow in gratitude and generosity. When we dwell in places where our stories and gifts are received, we are increasingly able to receive the stories of others and what they have to offer. We can include the contributions and gifts of others alongside others. It is not a competition of who gives how much or if one person's contribution seems more than another's. All contribute and work together, allowing the good we bring to transform our communities and others.

Finally, we remain curious: curious about God, about ourselves, about the world, and about others. We remain curious about God and how our salvation is continually being worked out as the Holy Spirit invites us to become more like Christ. We remain curious about ourselves through learning, growing, and seeing what is possible. This curiosity also keeps us in a posture of gentleness and hospitality toward ourselves. This gentleness toward ourselves expresses how we treat others and can be curious about them. We do this by asking questions and receiving the stories others share. A curiosity about the world includes creation, from the wind in our face to the ocean beyond our horizon. This curiosity delights in the playfulness of a puppy and grieves at the tragedy of forest fires. This curiosity makes way for patience; it means we can enjoy the present and the people God has brought. Continuing in this curiosity enables us to be people of welcome.

BELONGING

Belonging is a great longing of the human heart—a desire to be seen, known, and received. These places of true welcome tend to be hard to find. Our world moves at such a fast pace, and we have so much that demands our attention. But becoming a person of welcome means that we get to create these places for others: places where they are seen, heard, and received. We get to create places of beauty, depth, and being known. This work is costly, but worth it. So many people have been hurt by places of counterfeit hospitality. It is well worth creating places where beauty, goodness, generosity, and love flourish.

Sadly, churches can be places of counterfeit hospitality, requiring a person to leave the good gifts God gave them at the door. In becoming people of welcome, we can take welcome to those who can no longer walk into a church building but still long to belong. We can take them the love of Jesus, no strings attached, and provide them true welcome wherever they are.

The Spiritual Practice of Discernment

So many of us are looking for places and people of welcome. But understanding whether a community is truly welcoming requires discernment. This spiritual practice is the process of carefully discerning which way forward is right. It involves trustworthy voices, reflection on our lives, attentiveness to peace, and faith.

If you are seeking to discern a difficult question, consider walking through the following framework.

Trustworthy Voices

Trustworthy voices include Scripture, the Holy Spirit, mature Christians, and those who know you well. As you listen to these voices, look for alignment, echoes, contradictions, and candor. When there is alignment between God's voice and mature and faithful Christians who know you, this is a way forward to seriously consider.

Reflection

Reflecting on the past, present, and future gives us a panoramic view of our lives and God's ways of working. When we reflect on the past, we remember aspects of God we have forgotten, the ways of God's faithfulness, and the presence of people. These memories help to increase our faith and trust in the present and the future. Reflecting on the present keeps us grounded in realities that we need to attend to. Family, responsibilities, community, and more are a part of our discernment. As we look and imagine the future, we do so based on what is true from the past, what is real in the present, and what might be in the future.

Presence of Peace

In discernment, there is often the presence of peace This presence along with trustworthy voices, reflection, and faith can provide confidence in our discernment. Jesus promises us that the Holy Spirit will bring us peace—a peace that is sensed rather than explained, a peace that is evidence that God is with us wherever we go and whatever we decide. This peace can show up in heart, mind, body, and soul. Paying attention to each part of its presence, or lack, helps us in our discernment. If you are lacking peace, pause to pay attention as to why.

Faith

Finally, discernment requires faith. At some point, you must simply choose to move in a particular direction. This movement will demand faith and adventure; you will need to move toward both knowns and unknowns. This moment of faith is a step with God. He is with you no matter what.

5

HEALED HEARTS ARE HOSPITABLE HEARTS

FOR SOME REASON God has always had me in large institutions. From the city I grew up in, to the schools I attended, to the communities I worshiped in, I have always been in the big. As I served in these places, I found that charisma and going further kept them going. The leaders and people preferred charisma over character, going further over going deeper, and mind over heart. Anyone who slows others down gets pushed to the side.

To survive and serve, I kept my heart buried. Pushing my heart down, I let productivity lead. In the speed and success, I stopped seeing myself—and I stopped seeing the stranger. Gradually, the people I was called to serve started to be in the way; just as I didn't have time for my own heart, I didn't have time for their hearts.

After a very weary season with my heart buried deep, I stepped away from fast-paced productivity. God slowly began a recovery process in my heart, and it began to resurface.

Throughout the Old Testament, God invites his people to see the stranger, to welcome the stranger, and to care for the stranger in their land. As he does this, his plea is to remember what it was like for them to be a stranger—to remember their own pain and exclusion and, in doing so, to identify with strangers and to care for them (Leviticus 19:33-34; Exodus 23:9). When we have lost sight of our own stranger-like status, we often forget the strangers around us.

Christine Pohl says, "Deep sensitivity to the suffering of those in need comes from our ability to put ourselves in their position, and from remembering our own experiences of vulnerability and dependence. This sense of shared human experience extends even to those most foreign to us."

When I pushed my heart aside and became a stranger to myself, I couldn't see the strangers around me. But thankfully, Jesus always sees through to our hearts.

CUT TO THE HEART

Jesus was a master of seeing and cutting to the heart. He would pause with his presence and ask questions that would pierce straight and deep. Consider his encounter with a woman who has come to draw water from a well (John 4:1-26). She has not been completely rejected by her community, but likely isn't the bright hope for her community either. She is on the fringes. Jesus, resting from his journey, begins to banter with this woman around the well. It starts out practical, then goes theological. But then his questions cut to the heart. The woman's heart is exposed, but met by the one she longs for—Messiah. She immediately goes and tells her whole community about Jesus.

The story in John ends with unexpected multiplication: because of the woman's testimony, those in her town believed in Jesus. Because Jesus paused to be present, he met this woman's deepest longing for Messiah. And as a result, she told her entire town. They listened as she told her story. They then sought out the one who had met her with presence and salvation and invited him to stay. He saw, welcomed, and cut to her heart as she chose to share it. This vulnerability and healing led to many others knowing Jesus and having their hopes fulfilled.

Just as Jesus saw the woman, the woman saw Jesus. They both chose to dialogue and to ask for what they needed. Both made themselves vulnerable. Jesus did so by pausing by the well and asking for help. The woman chose to make herself vulnerable by engaging in conversation and being honest with a stranger. These actions of vulnerability took great courage, and their fruit was multiplied in the community. For us to emulate these actions requires that we remain vulnerable and courageous—and, like the woman, ask our questions. We remain open to Jesus, to ourselves, and to those around us.

THE POWER OF STAYING

Growing up as a next-generation immigrant, I was keenly aware of how different our family was from many of the families in our neighborhood. In addition to this cultural difference, my younger sister has Down syndrome. In the neighborhood, in school, and in the Armenian community, some treated our family differently because of her disability. I don't know that people intentionally did this. I imagine that they simply didn't know what to do. Even so, these small rejections, avoidances, and exclusions added up. We noticed and felt this when we were left out, looked past, and pushed aside. We were often moved to the outskirts of what was happening. Community wasn't easy to find in the neighborhood or in our cultural community.

The woman at the well also had a history of small rejections, avoidances, and exclusions. The text tells us that she had been married multiple times, and was living with a man who was not her husband. Commentators have often interpreted this to mean that she was an adulteress, shunned by her community. It may be more likely that she was divorced by her husbands, which would still be a recipe for being an outcast. What is noteworthy is that when she went back to her community to tell them about Jesus, they believed her. Lynn Cohick writes,

> The fact that the townspeople listen to her testimony suggests that she was not a shunned sinner. They believe Jesus is the Messiah not because of the disciples' preaching, nor because she allegedly changed her ways, for that would take time to validate. Rather, they believe because of her testimony. They probably knew she had religious questions and was not easily swayed by every preacher passing through. She was, therefore, a credible witness.

This woman had a history of rejection, but she also had a community that included her, knew her, listened to her, and was influenced by her. I don't know what it took for this woman to be included in her community. I don't know what it took for the community to trust, include, and believe her. What we can see is a mixture of pain, vulnerability, dependence, thoughtfulness, and care. We see pain from the woman's past. We see she had the vulnerability to open herself up to a community. We see she was dependent on a community when life didn't look like it should. We see thoughtfulness in her questions to Jesus and testimony to the community. And we see care that was exchanged between both the woman and the community. She cared enough to tell them about Jesus. They had been caring for her for a while, and they listened to her words. When our hearts are mutually seen and cared for, love, welcome, and transformation multiply. Yet, we often stop ourselves short from honest conversations with Jesus, ourselves, and our community.

My family stayed connected with certain people within our community. My mom found a few faithful friends within. My dad found a soccer team that would play every Sunday night. It was up close that they came to be known and to know, to receive and to offer care and friendship.

Knowing and experiencing what it takes to stay gives us understanding, empathy, and wisdom when we see the stranger and receive others.

RESISTANCE

Even as we want to stay or remain engaged, we often have inner resistance. This inner resistance hinders our ability to help a stranger or receive welcome from another. Resistance can be a warning indicator that we need to look at a situation with wisdom. Resistance can also be a teacher; it can show us parts of ourselves that need to be healed for us to be people of welcome where God has called us. My work as a spiritual director includes recognizing that resistance is normal and moving through the resistance together. Often, on the other side of resistance, we find freedom. And what we need to do is stay with Jesus and walk through it.

Resistance often shows up when we choose to hide, are stubborn in heart or head, or are wounded.

In hiding, we follow the pattern of our first mother and father, who hid themselves from God in their sin. Shame keeps us in hiding, whether it is because of our sin or the sin of another. When this happens, we need someone to come and find us. Jesus regularly comes to find us, but we must let him. We have the power to stay hidden when he longs to find us. Often, we hide by minimizing our pain. We hide by blaming ourselves, God, or others. We hide because we are afraid of what God will do or reveal.

Our stubbornness often has roots in habits that have kept our wounded parts safe from rewounding. All of us try to self-protect. We protect ourselves by numbing our pain, grumbling, and blaming. But all of these habits deflect Jesus and our loved ones from coming toward us. They harden our hearts to love, goodness, and grace.

We struggle, because we desperately want to be known—and are also afraid to be known.

At the root of a hard heart is a hurting heart. These hurting hearts are disconnected from others, from themselves, and from God. These hearts are suffering alone. In their book *Suffer Strong*, Katherine and Jay Wolf write, "A hard heart usually starts with a small hurt. A heart doesn't turn to stone overnight; it's a process of micro tears crystallizing with bitterness over time." If our hurts are a series of microtears, and maybe even some major ones, then we need a variety of helps: Band-Aids or surgery, time or medicine, a small first-aid kit or a hospital. We need many ways to sit with Jesus. We need a community that cares for us. We need the vulnerability and humility to receive the healing we need, so that our hearts might be able to see the stranger.

So, what do we do with our resistance? What do we do with our hiding, hard, and hurting hearts?

We remain connected to Jesus and a safe and healthy community. We do this by allowing ourselves to be seen and found, even if it is only by a few. We are not meant to be shallowly seen by many, but deeply by a few. This insight extends to our sin and our pain. We bring every tear, big or small, to Jesus. We allow Jesus to see and move into the depths of our hearts, so that we might be healed. We speak and share in community our pains, our questions, and our broken hearts. And we repeat.

Hearts do not harden overnight, but over time. If unattended, our hearts will continue to harden rather than heal. And healed hearts are the ones that live out the fullest hospitality. Healed hearts are able to see hurting hearts. Healed hearts are hospitable hearts.

THE TIME IT TAKES

My recovery from exhaustion in pastoral ministry took a long time, and it included a lot of people. Simply stepping away started the recovery process. Experiencing the beautiful outdoors, receiving the gift of friendship, playing, laughing, resting from more microtears—these were the first things that needed to happen. Another step was to cultivate as many reminders of God's goodness, faithfulness, and presence as I could. My community, the Scriptures, and time in solitude and silence helped bring these reminders to light.

I also had to regularly choose to face God and allow God to meet me. Many times, I didn't want to do that. I wanted to lick my wounds, stay in my complaints, and linger in blaming others. This cycle kept my heart buried; I was unable to see anyone else but myself. I was turned inward, when I needed to open myself outward to God. Over time and with conviction, I kept myself turned toward God in various ways. Through regular friendship, prayer, coaching, and serving others, I kept myself connected to others and myself. Through the practices of rest, spiritual direction, and daily examen, I stayed connected to myself and to

God. Through corporate worship, all these came together. Five years of this work, and I found myself strengthened and readied for greater heart and service.

At the beginning of this time of healing, it felt like I was sidelined from meaningful work. At times, I felt too wounded to be able to do things that mattered. I also wondered how long I would be sidelined. A few years later, reflecting on the past season, I was telling a good friend how I had felt sidelined, but was at last feeling ready to dream again. He chuckled and said, "Laura, only you would say this. I have watched you create and serve these past years. You weren't sidelined." His words gave me perspective. I was able to see God's goodness—to see that just because I was wounded and recovering didn't mean there wasn't meaningful work I could do. Our communities give us perspective. They help us see what we cannot see. They hold us when we need to be held. They heal us by walking with us. They teach us how to walk with others again. What a gift to have our communities.

The Spiritual Practice of Non-judgment

Our small and great hurts are personal, and we often think we have the best view of them. Yet our sight is limited, and the work of healing involves allowing God to see us and keeping ourselves in his sight.

Allowing God to see means that he touches the wounds and the weariness. It means that he meets us in our questions and our tears. Allowing God to see means that we stay unhidden, even though everything in us wants to cover up. Just as the Samaritan woman stayed with Jesus, we stay with him. And it is often in the times we most resist—when we most want to cover up or to run—that there is a breakthrough coming.

In order to keep hospitable hearts, we must have healed hearts. This means we regularly work to come out of hiding toward Jesus and others. This takes work. The good news is that this work does not begin with us. Jesus is, and has always been, the first to move toward us. He has also promised to be *with us* always (Matthew 28:20). Jesus does not demand that we move from our pain toward him; he promises that he has already moved toward our pain and meets us in it. Our work is to welcome him and welcome ourselves.

The following practice invites you to practice non-judgment of yourself and to hear the good things God has for you. One of the byproducts of this regular practice is greater grace toward others. The extension of empathy and compassion begin as you receive those things form Jesus. If possible, practice this three times a week for a month. Soak in the ways God is meeting you.

* Find a quiet place in solitude. Set aside fifteen to twenty minutes for this practice.

* Repeat the following verse aloud three times, taking a few seconds of pause between the readings:

  "Return to your rest, my soul, for the LORD has been good to you" (Psalm 116:7).

* Respond to the following questions:

  - In this moment, what are you most aware of in your physical body?
  - In this moment, what thought is most present to you?
  - In this moment, what choice (past, present, or future) is most loud right now?
  - In this moment, what emotion is strongest in you?

* Sit with your responses for at least one minute, and welcome every response. Refrain from judging yourself, critiquing your responses, or moving on from the present moment. Simply welcome each response as a communicator of where you are right now.

* Following this time of non-judgment, respond to the question, "How is it with my soul?"

* Sit with this response and welcome the state of your soul.

* It may be at peace; it may be disturbed. Maybe it is wrestling with something or is unsettled. It might be filled with hope and gratitude. Whatever your response, welcome your soul.

* After this time, open yourself up to God and allow God to meet and minister to you. He might remind you of a song, a Scripture, or maybe a certain tone or facial expression.

* If it is helpful, remember the ways that the Lord has been good to you.

* Close your time by returning to our opening verse: "Return to your rest, my soul, for the LORD has been good to you" (Psalm 116:7).

6

THE EXCHANGE OF GIFTS

For every gathering, there was a fully expected argument. When the end of the evening was nearing, my mom's best friend, Leila, would come into the kitchen and start washing dishes. My mom would exclaim, "Put those dishes down; you don't have to do them; we'll do them later!" Leila would keep washing and exclaim back, "No, I am washing these dishes. You get out of the kitchen." That banter would go back and forth a few rounds before someone eventually won. It happened every single time, without fail. The most persistent arguer won. Yet, in each of these robust rounds, no one was counting. It was simply what we did. There was no tally sheet to show who had paid last time or how many dishes had been washed. We kept no ledger of gifts given and received. We simply enjoyed the exchange of generosity.

OUR ECONOMIES

Some cultures and communities keep tighter ledgers than others. In some relationships, someone pays for a meal, and the other says, "I'll get it next time." In other relationships, when the waiter comes around, the group carefully splits the bill according to the items ordered. Think also of calculations around invitations:

when someone is invited to a wedding and it comes time for the other person's wedding, the other must be invited. Tight ledgers like these keep a list of debits and credits of transactions, amounts of time and money, as well as what is fair and unfair. The goal is balance. But is this the right goal?

The American culture of entrepreneurship, fueled by capitalism, has incredible benefits. Creativity, solutions, and generosity can come from this economy. But one dark side of this economy is that everything is a competition. Every interaction is logged in a ledger, and debits and credits are calculated even outside of the bank. For many of us, this mindset infiltrates what we say and do, who we spend time with, and how free we are to be generous and loving. This competitive, economical mindset can dictate to us even when we don't realize it. It is too easy for us to be bound by credits and debits, rather than living in the freedom of being guided by love and grace. The truth is that God's economy of grace is based on abundance and exponential resources such as love, forgiveness, and hope. These don't balance out cleanly. These resources are not based on the US market.

If we operate from debits and credits in this way, our mindset and actions may become competitive calculations rather than expansive graces. We should beware of calculating our actions in God's sight as well as in the eyes of others. It is unsettling when someone outgives or offers more to us than we can give. When we feel this unease, we should note that we may be bound to the tally sheet of debits and credits rather than grace and love.

JOURNEYING TOWARD GRACE

At the end of his Gospel, Luke shares the story of two travelers wondering what happened to their hopes for a savior. As they walk, they talk about the crucifixion of Jesus—and the death, with him, of everything they had hoped for. They carry their profound sadness over their lost hope that Jesus would be the Messiah. While they are walking, Jesus joins in their journey and conversation. He asks what they are talking about. They do not recognize Jesus. But they are surprised this person doesn't know what has happened; they explain all the weekend's events to him (Luke 24:14-24).

As the two followers traveled, they talked about the crucifixion and what the women saw. We can only imagine the details of their conversation. They may have repeatedly asked the same question, as if an answer would suddenly appear. Their conversation may have paused deeply for silence as their minds and hearts processed what they saw, heard, and took in. Their conversation might have included anger and tears, disappointments and doubts. We do know that "they were kept from recognizing him" (Luke 24:16). We do know what Jesus asked them: "What are you discussing together as you walk along?" (Luke 24:17). When they heard his question, they stopped dead in their tracks.

With sadness and confusion, they welcomed Jesus into the conversation, their expectations, and the reality of their sorrow and pain. As they gave space to this unrecognizable traveler, Jesus played ignorant and drew out their thoughts, feelings, and beliefs. He allowed them to recount what had happened, express their confusion, and offer their disappointment. Jesus gave them space to attempt to make sense of their circumstances. The answer to all they were hoping and looking for was before their eyes. But he didn't stop their searching, and he withheld his knowledge. Even as the men hosted Jesus physically, he hosted a space for their minds and hearts as they grieved and tried to make sense of their worlds. They were completely unaware.

SEEING CHRIST

The story continues as they approach their destination, and we see an exchange of gifts on the journey to Emmaus. Jesus' pause is a gift of space for the two travelers. Jesus continues as if he were going further, but they invite him to stay for the evening. Jesus accepts their welcome. And when they all sit to eat, Jesus takes the bread and gives thanks, breaks the bread, and passes it around. In this moment, the travelers recognize him—but he disappears. They are amazed, and remember together when their hearts burned from his teaching (Luke 24:28-32).

The two travelers practice hospitality as they seek to care for Jesus, a solo traveler on a dangerous road. Jesus receives the invitation, and just as the two travelers are the hosts, Jesus reverses the roles, taking the bread, blessing it, and giving it to them. The exchange of gifts takes place, and these two disciples now see the grace and gift that is before them—Jesus alive and their hopes fulfilled.

Theologian Amy Oden says of the exchange,

> Because the guest is actually more than just a guest, but is Christ, then there is another surprise as well. Christ becomes the host and the host becomes the guest. When we attend to the guest, we are not left unchanged. The Greek of the New Testament that is used to express hospitality carries within it the reality of shared identity and partnership. The same word, *xenos*, can mean guest, host, or stranger. The semantic fluidity conveys the blurred identities of guest and host, heightened by the recognition of Christ.

"When we attend to the guest, we are not left unchanged." Yes; the host has something for the guest, and the guest has something for the host. The exchange of gifts assumes that we have something for one another, but at its best, this exchange does not include competition or tally. When the exchange of gifts happens, we, with the disciples, see Jesus and one another in the fullness of beauty, grace, and goodness. We have gifts and graces for one another.

The travelers' story doesn't end when Jesus disappears. They immediately get up and return to Jerusalem: "The two told what had happened on the way, and how Jesus was recognized by them when he broke the bread" (Luke 24:35). The gifts and graces kept going.

THE EXCHANGE OF GIFTS

A few years ago, a man named Will joined a retreat I was hosting. A friend had invited Will, and I knew nothing about him. We gladly welcomed him. As part of my ministry, I was hosting monthly retreats, and Will began attending them regularly. He participated, shared, and invited other friends to join. I still didn't know much about Will, except that he regularly opened up to God. I was always glad to see him, and watched as he continued to lean in through moments of pain and uncertainty. A year after he started attending these retreats, Will made a generous donation to the retreat ministry.

Along with this donation, he unveiled the last year of his life to me. His wife of over thirty years had left him in November, before the pandemic hit. It was unexpected, and he found himself in a place of deep pain—confused by what was happening, trying to make sense of his present, and wondering what his future would hold. Unbeknownst to me and the other retreat hosts, the retreats held Will and his pain and confusion. He kept coming as God and people met him, journeying with him.

When I called him to thank him for his donation, he said, "Laura, for the first time in over a year, I finally feel that I have the ability to give and participate in the exchanging of gifts." When he said this I immediately sensed God's grace in Will's life and in my life. I was giving the space of the retreats. He was beginning to give out of his abundant means. And it didn't matter who seemed to be giving more; comparison didn't even enter our minds. We were both receiving grace. For the exchange of gifts is the exchange of grace.

HOSPITALITY IN THE MIDST OF SUFFERING

On the road to Emmaus, Jesus gave the two travelers the gift of conversation and presence in the midst of their suffering. When we expect God to be present in every interaction, especially in ones of need, we are offering a hopeful and generous gift to others. Consider the way that Jesus joins them in solidarity in his question to them, "Did not the Messiah have to suffer these things and then enter his glory?" (Luke 24:26). The two travelers are themselves suffering, and Jesus reminds them through the stories of their history that the Christ, too, was called to suffer. Having heard their pain, Jesus meets their suffering in the present with reminders of the past and hope for the future. Jesus does this for us today, and it is what we can offer others as well.

Christian neurobiologist Curt Thompson says, "In distress, the brain can do a lot of hard things as long as it doesn't have to do them alone." Two travelers are sharing their suffering and disappointment, and the God of the universe meets them in their suffering, informed by his own suffering. This is the generosity of hosting one another and exchanging the gifts of presence and care.

We never know what another is going through in the moment that we encounter them. With this in mind, along with the great grace we have been given, what would our hospitality look like if we expected God to be present in every interaction? What would it look like if we stayed present in the hard things people are walking through?

LEARNING TO GIVE AND RECEIVE

Over my years of pastoral ministry, I mastered what I call the pastoral pivot. (I claim I coined the phrase, but someone else probably has come up with it too.) The pastoral pivot happens when someone genuinely asks how you, the pastor or leader, are doing; you offer a quick quip, and then pivot back to the other person. Now, sometimes the pivot is appropriate; there are times when one is in the role of ministering and the other person needs primary attention. Yet there are always those around us who genuinely want to know how we are and care for us—despite our roles of service and leadership. For those of us who are regularly serving others, we often pivot, taking the attention and talk about needs off ourselves. We don't want to be a burden. Over my many years of practicing the pastoral pivot, I found very few spaces where I could be known. I had specialists who cared for me—doctors, spiritual directors, therapists, and mentors—but what I was lacking was friendships. In friendships, we carry one another and pour out whatever grace we have on each other. And reciprocal friendships don't keep a tally sheet.

When I stepped away from congregational pastoral ministry without a formal title or role, I started to relearn what it meant to give and receive in this exchange of hospitality. I didn't even know I needed this.

I remember one moment when we were being hosted by new friends, playing in the pool with our kids. I was relearning how to be myself, and I shared with my friend that I was relearning how to receive. His response was, "You are learning to be human again." His words hit me to my core. "You are learning to be human again." Learning to freely give and receive, to laugh without expectation, to surrender the pastoral pivot, and to be freely loved without a ledger. My friend's words have stayed with me since.

Some of us haven't felt our humanity in a long time. We have yet to experience the solidarity of friendship and care, a solidarity that isn't based on comparison but on our shared humanity and the grace we have received. In the fullness of his humanity, Jesus meets us in ours. He pours gifts and grace out to us, so that we might extend those gifts and graces to others.

The Spiritual Practice of Generosity and Humility

In hospitality, we get to practice the exchange of gifts. We suffer, serve, and join in solidarity with one another through these sufferings and celebrations. We are met by others and by our God, who shows up repeatedly. It is a beautiful chance to open up. The practices of generosity and humility lead us to meet each other, as we confidently expect that God is present with us.

We practice generosity in offering our gifts to another, understanding that they were first given to us. In humility, we generously extend what we have been given. God is faithfully present both when we serve others and when others serve us; thus, all are open to God's transformation.

So then, how do we practice generosity and humility with a posture of expecting Christ's presence?

Practicing generosity means we gaze outside of ourselves, and that we even look beyond the person before us. A generous gaze looks to the expectation that Christ is present with us. In generosity, then, we hold hope for what might be to come.

Practicing humility means we take a posture of honesty with our importance, not demeaning or elevating ourselves, but seeing ourselves as humans alongside other humans. In humility, then, we walk with others in their suffering and serve them.

We practice generosity by:

* Listening to learn from another
* Remembering that what we have was given by grace, and extending those gifts freely
* Celebrating victories with others, as well as holding hope for them when they cannot hold it for themselves

* Expecting God to be present in our interactions of hospitality

We practice humility by:

* Suspending judgment on another's situation or struggle
* Surrendering our comforts and entering the discomfort of another person
* Not assuming we know the pace of someone else's process

Generosity and humility work together in this human exchange of hope, grace, and gifts.

7

PREPARING YOURSELF

Sundays are for curveballs. And I'm talking about church, not baseball. When I was a pastor, the only thing that would save me from a Sunday morning curveball was preparation. When I sat down to go over the worship service, there was always an amendment, addition, or change to the lineup. (I'm not sure why I am using baseball metaphors, but they are working for me.) I was attentive during polite greetings between services, never knowing if they would turn into in-depth conversations. As a pastor, I wanted to serve in all the ways I could. I wanted to honor each moment I was a part of and each person I was with. To do this, I had to plan for what I knew so that I could be present with the unexpected.

My preparation included writing and practicing all worship leadership language the week before and the morning of. It included washing and drying my hair the evening before, and choosing my outfit and earrings (I won't engage the vast difference in physical preparation between male and female pastors). It also included sleeping early the evening before and waking up early Sunday morning. And it meant driving to the church separately from my family, so that I could have a time of quiet before hosting and welcoming others. This practice and preparation gave me mental space. It gave me confidence that when the unexpected came, I would be able to respond to it with a presence that met the moment and the person. I was grateful when I could do so.

There's a popular saying, "We don't rise to the level of our expectations; we fall to the level of our training." In other words, we don't "rise to the occasion," as the cliché goes. We don't jump to a greater ability level when something unexpected comes up. We fall to the level of our training—to what we have practiced doing. When it comes to hospitality, what does it mean to train? How do we train?

PRACTICE WELCOME BY RECEIVING IT

We practice welcome by receiving it. We prepare by receiving hospitality and allowing ourselves to breathe. If you don't know how to be hosted in a space, how to take a deep breath, you won't be able to do that for another.

In 2020, I started a ministry called Digital Silent Retreats. As the world was sheltering in place, and churches paused in-person worship services, many people were struggling to find their rhythms with God. I was struggling, too. I designed a retreat opportunity for others that included time on Zoom, solitude and silence with a retreat guide built on the spiritual practices, and a closing time with retreat participants sharing stories of how God had met them.

As these retreats grew, I invited other trusted coaches and spiritual directors to join me as hosts. In the training for the Digital Silent Retreat ministry, I require each host to practice receiving before hosting others. They do so by going through the retreat guide and the spiritual practices they are asking others to go through. Through this practice, the hosts allow Jesus to minister to them before they minister to others. Often, if we as hosts and leaders do not allow ourselves to be ministered to first, we will unknowingly require that our guests minister to us.

You may be wondering if it matters that we receive. Sure, Jesus went away to pray, but isn't giving more important than receiving?

Herein lies a hidden danger of hosting. We sometimes use our service as a cover for control. When we host, we wield more power than we know—and are quite comfortable with that. We use service, giving, and hosting as a way to comfort and soothe ourselves. Ouch. It's true.

When we learn to receive, we practice laying down our power, laying down our impulse to control and command. We sit with this discomfort so that when another comes to us and we find ourselves uncomfortable, we are willing to sit with our discomfort and be present to that person. Parker Palmer says,

> One of the hardest things we must do sometimes is to be present to another person's pain without trying to "fix" it, to simply stand respectfully at the edge of that person's mystery and misery. Standing there, we feel useless and powerless. In an effort to avoid those feelings, I give advice, which sets me, not you, free.

Hospitality invites anxiety. We become anxious because of performance, presentation, vulnerability, rejection, and acceptance. Being hospitable means we are at the mercy of another's response. We need our identity and the practice of receiving God's goodness, love, confidence, and words to be deeply rooted in us. Otherwise, when we offer hospitality, we'll find our anxiety taking up the air in the room. Our concerns about what people think will lead us to manipulate. We will not allow others to be free because we have not been set free.

We receive that we might be free. We receive that we might offer freedom to another.

When we prepare ourselves by receiving, we surrender power and gain freedom. When we prepare ourselves by slowing down, we live into the reality of our dependence on and security in Jesus. When we prepare ourselves by allowing the Spirit to lead us in quiet, we know we are cared for and can trust the Spirit to care for the other through us.

To receive our identity as beloved, we must be able to receive from God and be present with God.

ALWAYS ATTACHED

We are all attached to something. Something has worked for us; something has gotten us through hard times. For many of us, these attachments are hard to see. A variety of things have worked to carry us. Some attachments are very good things—family, friendship, God, beauty, creativity, work, and more. God has given us good ways to be dependent and interdependent. But there are also attachments that are not good. Often, these attachments revolve around identity and image. And identity and image tend to show up in what we own and how we perform.

As a spiritual director, I have a spiritual director supervisor. I call her a soul surgeon. The goal of our supervision time is to pay attention to what is going on in me that hinders me from being present and of service to directees. We explore these issues through a verbatim—a practice of walking through a conversation line by line and paying attention to what was happening in the situation. I believe it is from one of the circles of hell. Bad theology aside, these verbatims allow my supervisor and me to examine the context when something hindered me from serving the directee. She asks questions with her sterilized and sharpened tools, and surgery begins.

One of my frequent hindrances is wanting the directee to have an *aha* moment or a breakthrough. I long for them to see and hear from God in a way that meets them in the deepest parts of their souls. This longing is not a wrong desire or longing. These moments are beautiful! What is not good is when I push the pace or grow impatient with the other person's journey and want a breakthrough—not for their sake, but because I think it reflects whether I am a good director worthy of my pay. The part of me that loves productivity and growth gets in the way of the directee before me. In those moments, I am not hosting the other but am soothing my ego, which needs forward movement to feel better about itself.

Another way attachment to our image shows up is in the excellence of hospitality. Some of us have narrowly defined hospitality by specific kinds of places: big, spotless, updated buildings in great locations. If we don't have that type of place, then our insecurities lead, and we assume we cannot be hospitable. Now, there is nothing wrong with beautiful and updated spaces that wow us, but we often conflate what we own with our ability to be hospitable. This attachment shows up as we demand perfection—excellent presentation, perfect placement, and flawless details.

Yet perfection often gets in the way of presence. Perfection drives some hosts. It exhausts me. I have lost count of the times I have expressed gratitude that social media and platforms like Pinterest didn't exist when I got married. We all miss out when we are wrapped up in images of excellence rather than invitations to presence. What does it matter if everything is perfect but the host isn't present to their guests? What does it matter if someone comes to worship on Sunday morning, but we can't pause and be present to them? And what gifts are we offering when we rush past the stories of our sons and daughters, the meaningful moments of our parents, and the stranger's needs? It is not only the guests that miss out, but also the hosts. In chasing perfection, we lose the joy of the moment.

HOW WE LIVE

You may be feeling some tension at this point in the chapter. Perhaps you long for Jesus to meet you; perhaps you see attachments that bind you. How do you move forward?

Jesus surrendered power and trusted God. He often slowed down to strengthen his identity in his Father. And he prepared for his work to come. He practiced with others, walking and teaching them to live in these ways as well. We also follow these ways of Jesus as we do the following:

* *We surrender power and trust the Spirit.* We surrender power as we lay down the thought that we are the first and only hosts. We surrender the power of transformation to the Holy Spirit.

* *We slow down and find security in Jesus.* We slow down to recognize that our pace is not rooted in the pace and presence of Jesus. We notice when performance, perfection, or productivity are driving us, and we choose to look to Jesus for our identity and security.

* *We prepare and practice.* The very practical piece of our hospitality is in our preparation and practice. We prepare so that details don't distract us from the unexpected. And we practice so that we keep learning how to receive and offer hospitality.

The Spiritual Practice of Centering Prayer

We can allow God to prepare us through the practice of centering prayer. Remember that we do not do spiritual practices for the fruit they bear, but for receiving the presence of God, for being with Jesus. Henri Nouwen beautifully describes this invitation to receive in prayer: "The real 'work' of prayer is to become silent and listen to the voice that says good things about me. To gently push aside and silence the many voices that question my goodness and to trust that I will hear the voice of blessing—that demands real effort."

The spiritual practice of centering prayer invites us to let go of our hard-work mentality, choosing to become silent. It helps us bring ourselves to a posture of listening to what God says. In centering prayer, you do not speak; you practice centering and recentering your mind on the truth of God so that there is space to hear God's voice.

As you enter this practice, trust in Scripture and instruction and the saints who have gone before you. Trust that God is ready to speak good, freedom, and blessing. Plan to practice centering prayer for ten to fourteen days, as this small practice relies on the consistent practice of being present to God.

Read the instructions as many times as you need to grasp the basics of the practice. It is okay to struggle through, especially the first few times (and even later)! This is why we call these methods *practices*—you are practicing them, and there will be some adjustment time.

* First, find a time and place of quiet and solitude where you know you will not be interrupted.

* Then, choose a short Scripture passage. Psalm 23 and John 1:1-14 are good places to start.

* Read the Scripture passage two to three times and choose a word or phrase that stands out. Hold this word or phrase in your mind; it will center and recenter you as you pray. You can put down the rest of the Scripture passage, as you will not return to it in prayer.

* Set a ten-minute timer with a quiet alarm, and sit in a comfortable position.

* You will spend the entire ten minutes of prayer in silence and quiet. Close your eyes if that is helpful. As you sit, focus on the word or phrase from the Scripture. Inevitably, your mind will be distracted; when it does, go back to the word or phrase and remember it again to center your mind on God's truth and open yourself up to God's presence.

* Continue in silence, recentering over and over until the timer goes off.

* When the alarm rings, take a few moments to come out of the silence and reflect on your time in centering prayer. Rest in the time you had, and express gratitude to God.

* Something may have come forth during your prayer. Maybe you felt an echo from something God has said before; perhaps you enjoyed God's presence. Maybe you just made it through. Feel no pressure to have an epiphany or a dramatic result. Centering prayer is about opening yourself up, recentering yourself when distracted, and welcoming God's presence.

* Rest in the time you had and express gratitude to God however you'd like.

As mentioned earlier, continue this practice daily for ten to fourteen days. Pay attention to anything that arises in you during centering prayer and throughout your days. You might notice a shift in your posture toward others. Ask God what he wants you to do with anything he has said or brought up. He may be calling you to deeper prayer or action.

Throughout, offer gratitude to God for speaking to you, treasure his word in your heart, and let Scripture transform your mind, heart, and hands in its time. Let the outcome and fruit of this practice rest with God.

CULTIVATING VISION

8

THE TOUR COMPANY HAD MISJUDGED THE MILES. What we thought would be a twelve-mile walk turned into sixteen, and the accompanying rain didn't help. We trekked all the miles—plus the bonus miles—until we arrived at an oceanside hotel. At this point, all I wanted was ice cream.

Upon checking in, I asked the receptionist where I could get some ice cream. She told me the connecting café served it. And then she said, "Leave your luggage here, buy your ice cream, and come back and take it upstairs to your room overlooking the Ría de Vigo. You are the only person in your group to have a view of the water. And don't tell anyone I gave you this room."

The receptionist knew her hotel and she had a vision of what it could provide. She knew a tired pilgrim when she saw one, and she had a plan of action ready. When I checked out, she was there again. She gave me a wink when I said, "Gracias."

WHAT IS TO COME

Hospitality includes a vision of the spaces we hold, the people who might come, and our guests' potential needs for their journey ahead. The kind receptionist knew her space and what it could provide, and she was able to meet the needs of the people who walked into her lobby. To be people of welcome, we must cultivate vision.

Jesus had vision when he ate his last meal with his disciples, knowing what was to come for him as well as for them. He shared his vision when he took the bread and the cup with thankfulness and gave it to his disciples, telling them that it represented his body and the promise of his covenant of salvation (Mark 14:22-25).

Jesus knew what was ahead for the disciples. Through this meal, Jesus met and nourished them for the road ahead. But while he was caring for his disciples on that night, he was also extending the table to many in the future. Today, each time we come to the Lord's Table, we are coming to a well-thought-out and prepared table. We receive a reminder for the day and provision for our needs in the days to come. We get to experience this hospitality over and over again.

Yet, even as Jesus held the vision for this last meal, many others worked toward it. The master of a certain house had his large upper room "furnished and ready" (Mark 14:15). Jesus had told his disciples to go find the room and make the preparations there. At his instructions, "the disciples left, went into the city and found things just as Jesus had told them. So they prepared the Passover" (Mark 14:16).

And, even before Jesus told the disciples to prepare a room, a woman had offered him a costly gift, anointing him for his burial (Mark 14:1-11). She anticipated his need; perhaps she had heard Jesus' words about his coming death. She saw what he would need and provided it. Her story reminds us that Jesus didn't carry his vision alone. Others saw his vision and joined in the work of hospitality. Each person's work built upon one another: the costly sacrifice, the extravagant room ready for hospitality, and the nourishment of a table for all who would come. All this work, combined, expanded hospitality from one person to a dozen people—and, at last, to the whole world.

PAST PREPARERS

As I write this chapter, I am sitting in a repurposed barn outside of Philadelphia—a space for retreats where people gather to be with God and one another. My hosts have prepared everything that I might need for a few days of writing. When I arrived, the owners greeted me with warmth, welcome, and connecting stories. They showed me the light switches and told me where to walk by the creek. They told me where they imagined I would spend most of my time writing and where I might walk in the garden. Everything was prepared for my arrival, aligned with my specific purpose of writing. The owners' vision of having a space for family gatherings and for people to retreat, receive, and meet with God led the transformation and preparation of this space. It cost them something to make this space ready. I cannot imagine all the details that the owners considered when creating this space for its purpose.

Others prepared this space even before the new owners came to this place. The woman who owned the land before my current hosts had prepared the garden, and one of the requirements for buying the land was tending the garden. She had cultivated the garden, and knew that this space was worth continuing. Before the garden, the land served as a dairy farm, which nourished the community near and people afar with good milk. This nourishment provided what families needed for their work.

As we look for God's vision in tending to a space in the present, we should consider what the space was prepared for beforehand. This dairy farm is no longer an operating farm that provides nourishment through milk. Yet, it is still providing nourishment; it nourishes community, fellowship, retreat, and beauty. It nourishes the heart, mind, body, and soul.

Even as Jesus was preparing a table for his disciples and the church to come, a woman was preparing Jesus for his future, giving him what he needed for his journey. A space is not stagnant, existing only for a moment in time. Rather, it exists in multiple moments, each building upon one another.

THE COST OF PARTICIPATION

Even as people participated in the work of Jesus, it was costly. This work came with criticism. In the story of the woman who anointed Jesus, the Gospel writer relates that those present criticized her for the use of her perfume; they thought there was a better use for it. They rebuked her harshly. Jesus responded by telling them to leave her alone and naming her act beautiful. He told them that she did what she could, that she had prepared him for his work to come, and that her act would be remembered (Mark 14:4-9).

Participating in hospitality costs something. We may be judged for it. Yet, it is vital for what is to come.

The woman's service cost her something great. She willingly put herself in a vulnerable position both financially and socially. Yet she could see something beyond that the others in the room could not. She saw ahead and decided it was worth the cost to herself.

Our hospitality costs us something, and, so often, we want to know whether that something is worth the cost. Sometimes, we see purpose or hope. Sometimes, we don't.

THE REDEMPTION OF SPACES

The disciples made assumptions about the history of the woman who anointed Jesus' head. The disciples were quick to judge the woman's sacrificial action (Mark 14:4-5). They assumed they knew the cost of her actions and could use her possessions better than she could. But in being so quick to criticize, they were hindering themselves from seeing the big picture: her preparation of Jesus' work. We often make this same error when we watch the actions of others and assume we know their histories. Sadly, many of us may have harmed people both within and outside the church with quick accusations and misunderstandings.

This woman boldly entered a space and took a costly action. Jesus honored, defended, and protected her; he could see her offering for the gift that it was. By anointing him, she was not only breaking open a jar, but making room for her character and her community to be redeemed. After the disciples' ridicule, Jesus corrected them and reestablished what was most important—her offering. She was preparing Jesus for his death, readying what was needed in that moment and for the cross to come. She was also opening a space for Jesus to redeem her, redefine her action, and transform the disciples. This jar of nard cost the woman a financial and social price. It cost the disciples their pride. And it signaled the beginning of Jesus' costly journey to the cross. We must offer our past actions and our present circumstances to be broken open. Only when they are transformed and redeemed by Jesus can we offer them for hospitality. And all of us will pay the costs when something is broken open.

As we envision what hospitality we will provide in a given space, whether a city street or a church building, we should be aware of what that space has held beforehand. Some spaces have held beauty and life, much like the dairy farm. And some spaces have held pain, injustice, and suffering. We cannot ignore a place's history, but we can be a part of redeeming it with a new vision.

The team at Equal Justice Initiative is doing just that. This legal advocacy group is breaking open minds and hearts through what they call Legacy Sites, which are part of a national effort to create new memorials addressing the ongoing legacy of slavery, lynching, and racial segregation. These Legacy Sites are located in Montgomery, Alabama, a state where evidence of slavery and injustice remains and where justice reform is still greatly needed. The toil and cost of this good work affects heart, mind, body, and soul. Long hours, heartbreaking stories, and rigorous analysis of documents and evidence take a toll. But to those breaking their costly jars and opening their minds and hearts in places of injustice, it is worth it. They have courage in seeking their greater purpose. And when our courage and God's capacity meet, there is the possibility that God will redeem both places and people. When we prepare places for hospitality, we make possible both our own transformation and the transformation of others.

Sadly, the church—both its physical buildings, and its communities of people—has been a place of pain and injustice for many. (I refer to both a church's building and its people in the word *church*.) In the church, wrongs have been ignored, authorities have not been held accountable for their actions, and deep wounds have not been repaired. Things have been swept under the rug for the sake of moving forward and keeping peace. All of us involved in the church have a part to play in making repairs. We can help bring to light these cowardly actions in the face of dark realities. We can acknowledge the past together. And as our communities repair church buildings and institutions, we can be people of welcome. We can step out into the world as reminders of God's welcome, carrying the truth that each person has a home with God.

Preparing a space for hospitality may cost us more than anticipated. We may have to be courageous in ways we didn't anticipate.
If we lack purpose or vision, this can leave us embittered and
weary. But with a vision, we can consider the gain greater than our
cost, understanding the sacrifice to be worthy. And with purpose,
we find ourselves available to surrender what we hold on to for
the greater call—our calling to love the other. Preparing a place
costs everyone something. It cost Jesus everything.

My new friends in Philly are providing physical space for retreat. So many loving people have nourished this place for years.
As hosts continue places of hospitality, guests receive welcome on
their journey. When we rest in these places—being met by God
through others—we find redemption, hope, healing, joy, connection, creation, and so much more. God meets us on our
journey every step of the way, and our work is to prepare places
however and wherever God is calling us. We don't always know
who will show up or how they will do so, but we can prepare a
place for them.

The Spiritual Practice of Developing and Discerning Vision

To envision hospitality requires surrendering our agendas and preferences to what God might have in store. We open ourselves to this imagination in community. This community includes those who will be involved and those to whom this vision matters. This community should also comprise a range of people with voices and perspectives that might change our pace or make us face our hidden agendas. A collective imagination looks to God and asks, "What might be?" Often, the collective imagination shows up in a picture of how the community wants people to feel from the beginning to the end of an experience. It takes time to reach a place of vision that resonates with the heart, mind, body, and soul. But when the community arrives at this vision, the group is prepared to carry out the vision at all costs.

Through the practice of imagination, we cultivate a place for vision to unfold. Our minds open up through the stories we hear and the images we see—what I call "pictures of possibility." These can be actual stories we read, or those we make up. They can be places we see, or imagined places of welcome. The imagination opens up when we visit places and experience new things. Often, we get new ideas from seeing how another person or culture operates.

There are endless ways to open ourselves up to imagination, so I will offer just a few here. This exercise is geared toward an individual, but can also be practiced with a group of people. As you imagine, include God in your wanderings and spaces.

Start from Where You Are

First of all, start from where you are. Imagine a place where you feel most welcomed by God. This place can come from the past or the present. Try not to move into the future—that's not where you are. This place of welcome should feel like a place where you can be yourself without judgment and be received with great joy. It should allow you to be the most courageous and cared-for version of yourself. It can be a place with four walls or an endless horizon. Wherever it is, spend some time in this place.

Name What You Long For

As you come to this place, what do you most long for? You may long for a place of rest or protection. You might long for courage or the next challenge. Maybe you long for human connection and warmth. You might long to be a part of something bigger than yourself. What do you most long for as you continue to imagine this place?

Who Might Be Coming?

Shift your imagination now to those you imagine you might be hosting. Bring them into your imagined place. What do you imagine happening when they arrive?

What Do They Long For?

Why might they be coming? Are they looking for rest or protection? Are they longing for courage and need others to be courageous with them? Maybe they are longing for social connection and warmth. Could they desire to be part of something bigger than themselves? As you imagine them with you, what might they long for?

What Can You Provide?

Now, consider what you or your group can provide. Remember, this might be something costly to each of you. As you consider what God wants you to provide for them, the cost might naturally rise in the form of resistance or sadness. What can you or your group provide?

Name and Face Your Resistance with God

What resistance or sadness is coming up in you? How is this resistance or sadness pointing to what it might cost you? Sit with this possible cost and take your resistance and sadness to God in prayer, expressing candidly what you are thinking and feeling. As a group, express what this might cost you.

Discern the Cost

Next, discern whether any of the costs are what God is calling you to give up for the sake of those coming. Not all potential costs are required, yet being ready to surrender even before it is asked will help prepare you for hospitality and welcome. Allow the conviction of calling to emerge.

Turn Imagination into Vision

Return to the picture of the type of space and what you or your group might provide. What is the purpose of the people coming, and what is God calling you to provide? What does it look and feel like? It might need to be honed as you or your group practice, but you are off to a great start. Continue to practice being aware of the cost and any resistances so you can be mindful as you move toward this vision.

Move Forward with Joy

Prepare the space and place. Keep learning as you go. Carry your vision in mind, and stay open to the people who will be a part.

9

NECESSARY BOUNDARIES

Everyone cries on their wedding day. I was told this moment would come, and I anticipated it as my wedding day approached. And then it happened. My family was staying with a dear family friend, Cookie, for the wedding weekend; they had come to the church early for pictures and all the preceremony details. They had told Cookie, an older widow, that they would return to pick her up before the wedding. Her home was over thirty minutes from the church, and the city was unfamiliar to my family. My soon-to-be husband, Craig, saw my dad in the church parking lot, getting into his car forty-five minutes before the ceremony was to begin.

Unlike many Anglo-American weddings, which start at the time on the wedding invitation, Armenian weddings begin whenever the Armenians are ready. Craig quickly asked my dad where he was going. When my dad said he was going to pick up Cookie, Craig wisely told him to wait a moment to check with me. As my mom and I were fixing my veil, my dear friend in the house party peeked into the room and said, "Laura, your dad says he needs to go pick up Cookie, and Craig doesn't know what to tell him."

I quickly exclaimed, "But my dad has to walk me down the aisle in forty-five minutes. He can't go!"

My mom promptly replied, "Laura, she is our guest! We have to give her a ride to the ceremony!"

Cue tears. Cue an exchange of words. And cue my good friend coming to the rescue by saying, "I'll go get her for you." Problem solved. Cookie would be honored, and the wedding would start on American time. Our voices settled, but our hearts were still in the moment.

In that moment, two values came crashing. One for guests and one for time. One that valued hundreds of people and the clock, and another that valued one person, an honored guest. Values clashing: this is the tension of boundaries.

Values are at the heart of boundaries—spoken values, sometimes, but mostly unspoken ones. These unspoken values make boundaries even trickier and more likely to clash. My mom and I never talked about what was most important: starting on time, honoring the guest, or which guest to honor. The only way we knew there were boundaries was through conflict. And when we dig deep, we can see our values at play.

Before we discuss values, we need to address an issue. Boundaries seem completely antithetical to hospitality. How can someone be hospitable if they won't let someone in? And how can a church or Christian be seen as loving and welcoming if it has boundaries?

Christine Pohl says,

By definition, hospitality is gracious and generous. Limiting hospitality seems to undermine what is fundamental to the practice. But boundaries are also a problem because so many of them are hidden. Because Christian hospitality reflects divine hospitality, when it fails, it is especially devastating.

Here's the predicament: hospitality seems like something other than hospitality if it has boundaries. And then, there's a double whammy. Those boundaries are often hidden so no one knows when they are crossing them. But when people cross the boundaries, they face significant consequences. What do we do with this? We practice clarity.

CLARITY IS KIND

Years ago, I was asked to serve as the chapel speaker at a seminary. I knew this seminary had a more conservative position on women in leadership than I do. Previous women asked to speak had caused a stir; they were considered harsh in their words and were accused of bringing an agenda. The chaplain putting together the chapel schedule was mandated to bring in diverse voices, but at the same time, he had to make sure those voices knew the boundaries. Not very welcoming, but honest.

To make matters even more interesting, the chaplain told me that I couldn't use my title of reverend or pastor, and that I wasn't to preach but to bring an update on my ministry. When he listed this last boundary, I had to chuckle. I said, "You want me to bring a sermon—because if I bring an update on my ministry, then I have to talk about baptizing my daughter, preaching sermons, and having the title of pastor." He said, "Okay." I prayed about whether to accept this invitation. I even encouraged him to call his daughter-in-law, a good friend of mine, to vet me. She told him I was trustworthy. Many of you reading this right now would say, "Run!" I don't blame you. I would likely say the same thing.

The way he approached me, the boundaries he set for me, and his dishonor in not using my earned title and position were unjust to me and many others. Yet he was clear. This clarity allowed me to decide whether I would accept the invitation and how it was offered. It also allowed me to be more confident about God's invitation to show up and serve the students, faculty, and staff. I went because I wanted to serve the people there, and that was more important to me than our disagreement on the boundaries.

Imagine he had been unclear, and I didn't know all this context. What would happen when he didn't honor all those things that were true of me when I started to preach? How frustrating and harmful would it have been to not know the boundaries, to cross them, and face negative consequences? Even though our values didn't align, knowing the boundaries allowed me to honor God and to love the students well. I did preach that sermon, and it was a joy to love those students in that way. The chaplain thanked me. Because we each understood our clear boundaries, we could honor the work and people we were called to.

BOUNDARIES PROTECT

Spoken boundaries provide clarity and protection. They hold the purpose of the encounter, the gathering, or the service of the other. And in protecting purpose, they ultimately protect people.

We find Jesus protecting people by clarifying purpose in the Gospel of John. He names his purpose as a gatekeeper—a shepherd whose sheep know his voice (John 10:4). He extends protection to those who enter through his gate, knowing his voice.

John tells us that "Jesus used this figure of speech, but the Pharisees did not understand what he was telling them" (John 10:6). So, Jesus restates his illustration, going on to describe himself as the good shepherd who lays his life down for the sheep. He does this according to his authority as the Son of God.

As the gatekeeper, Jesus' purpose is to protect the sheep from thieves and robbers. In the world we all long for, there are no thieves and robbers. In the world we hope for, there is only welcome and love. Yet this is not the world we live in. Given this reality, there needs to be purpose and protection.

I wonder if boundaries create internal conflict because we long for a place where all are free and welcome without fear of harm, yet we cannot have that. We long to be a welcoming people and welcome others, knowing that there can be no harm done—yet we cannot avoid harm. Our hearts are set for a new heaven and a new earth where everything is made right and whole, but this reality is not here yet.

Good boundaries protect purpose and people. Every small and large community, bordered and unbordered country, and gated and ungated home will have a contextualized understanding of these good boundaries and their protection of purpose and people. Boundaries are complex conversations as they involve people, compassion, clarity, purpose, values, and context. And they are conversations worth having for the sake of those God calls us to serve.

NO FREDDIE FREELOADERS

Two Australian brothers run my favorite Texas coffee shop. They serve the best coffee and have no Wi-Fi. They also have the sparsest furniture—guests sit on unfinished, hard, wood stools. I repeat, they have no Wi-Fi. These values contradict the feeling we often want in a warm and inviting coffee shop, a cozy space to sit for a while and do some work. But that is because this is not their purpose. When I asked the brothers about this, one of them shared the purpose of their coffee shops: finding respite in your day. Therefore, in addition to the lack of Wi-Fi, the brothers hang signs that say "No Freddie Freeloaders" and "Short Stays Only." You'd think this coffee shop would be the most inhospitable place ever, yet it is one of the most hospitable coffee shops I have been to. No matter what, if one of the brothers is there when I visit, I get a personalized hello and a hug; warmth is exuded in both conversation and coffee. They bring hospitality through making good coffee, knowing their guests, keeping their vision clear, and being purposeful in their boundaries and care.

The owners have taken the time to name their values, hold clear boundaries, and focus on caring for people. Doing these things help them acknowledge their limits. When asked to provide coffee service for a large church's Easter Sunday, they declined the business. They knew they could not provide that amount of coffee and still live out their purpose. Who would turn down that kind of business? These brothers.

None of us can focus on everything. Naming what God wants us to value clarifies our purpose in expressing hospitality. This clarity allows us to align our actions with who we say we are. When we lack clarity on values and boundaries, we will find tension and confusion; when we forget boundaries, we will sacrifice our purpose and the chance to meaningfully engage. When we lack courage to align our values, the result will be pain and mistrust. Knowing, naming, clarifying, remembering, and acting on values are not primarily for getting everything right. We do this to remain aimed toward the good purpose that individuals and communities are called to.

Canon Caroline Westerhoff, a consultant to the Alban Institute, says,

> Predictable and consistent boundaries of time, place, and all the rest serve to reduce anxiety and confusion in any given

system, whether class, family, or church. They help to establish an environment in which tough and difficult work can go on, work for which the outcome is less than certain.

Within hospitality good and challenging work can happen. But we can only do this good work within boundaries.

My Aussie friends have aligned their work with their values, and it costs them. Yet they are reaching their goal of providing respite in the middle of the day. They are not dispensers of endless coffee, but caretakers of people's days. I imagine it is not easy to say no to major business opportunities, but they still do. These boundaries allow them to continue in the good and hard work of providing respite in a busy and weary community.

Most of us want to do what God has called us to do. We want our churches and communities to be light and love to others. Boundaries help establish environments of stability and security so that good work might happen. They enable the work of my Aussie friends, who are creating respite in a highly driven city for people who desperately need it.

ARTIFICIAL BOUNDARIES

Each follower of Jesus is called to practice hospitality (Romans 12:13; Hebrews 13:2; 1 Peter 4:8-9). Yes, each follower—not only those with the gift, time, means, or propensity. Each one of us is called to practice hospitality in the ways and to the places and people God has called us to. The entire body of Christ is needed! But too often, we put the extras on top. If we can't meet in person, we assume there can't be hospitality. We say, "I don't have the gift of hospitality," but we mean, "I don't have a big house, money, or means to throw a party." Or if we're honest, we might mean, "I don't want to take the time to offer hospitality." We compare, criticize, and cut ourselves off from offering hospitality to another. We put artificial boundaries on hospitality and hinder what might be possible.

My own home is not a place people usually ask to host in; nor is it where you might think a hospitable person lives. We live in a central city suburb. Our flooring consists of six different varieties, two dogs have run over our carpet, and our landscaping resembles a mud pit. The homes that are always asked to host a gathering have the most updated kitchens, and yards which could hold a wedding reception. Each time we talk about hosting others for a party or meal I immediately go through my checklist of problems: not enough space, horrible flooring and cabinets, dogs, and small space. Yet when I can move past my comparisons and artificial boundaries, I find that our guests are quite comfortable in our home. They lounge easily, linger at the dinner table, and comment the following day about the meaningful time they had.

Having an appealing physical space for hospitality is easier for some than others. But hospitality isn't only about the space; it is about the people who extend welcome in whatever space they are in. Each of us can be people of welcome, wherever we host. It takes practice to regularly release our own demands and artificial boundaries, and to cultivate a posture of hospitality that extends warmth, welcome, and care to others.

THE BOUNDARIED SHEPHERD

When we work to move past comparison and remove artificial boundaries, we are then able to identify necessary boundaries with more clarity and conviction. Often we need to set boundaries simply because of the capacity of the space or the host. There are only a certain number of guests you can feed, or number of stories you can hold. These boundaries can be hard to hold; we want to extend compassion and care, but we are limited by our capacity. We are then misunderstood; people may think we lack hospitality or care. However, these boundaries are an expression of care and compassion. We are simply limited.

In order to maintain boundaries with compassion and care, we must hold them with clarity and alignment. If our boundaries toss like the waves, people might see us as unreliable, playing favorites, or unjust. Clarity and alignment protect our vision and call to care. The best example I know is Jesus himself. Jesus knew his purpose. He extended care, yet he limited himself in solidarity with humankind. God chose to have limits and boundaries. He confined himself to a human body, and surrendered himself to injustice, hostility, and death. Even as he is the greatest host, he knows what it is like to be the most rejected. Paul reminds us of Jesus' humility, conviction, and compassion, saying of him,

> Who, being in very nature God,
>> did not consider equality with God something to be
>>> used to his own advantage;
> rather, he made himself nothing
>> by taking the very nature of a servant,
>> being made in human likeness.
> And being found in appearance as a man,
>> he humbled himself
>> by becoming obedient to death—
>>> even death on a cross! (Philippians 2:6-8)

Jesus takes his job as host more seriously than we ever could. He lived boundaried so that we might be welcome. He did so with humility, justice, and sacrifice. When we are clear on our values, purpose, and care for people, we do the good work of hospitality—hospitality that creates space for strangers and friends. Good boundaries are hard work, and they are worthy work. May we hold them with clarity and humility. May we hold them in alignment with the purposes God has for us.

The Spiritual Practice of Boundaries

As we explored in this chapter, we must hold boundaries with both strength and compassion. It is important to identify which boundaries need to be strong and which need to be soft, as well as which boundaries are yours to enforce.

In *humility*, we practice the boundary of knowing what we can or cannot provide. In *conviction*, we practice the boundaries of clarity and purpose. And in *compassion*, we practice the tenderness of care that sees people despite our limitations.

As you consider each of these characteristics, start with a known context you regularly inhabit. You can do this as an individual or with the group you serve with. With this known context, consider:

* The people God is calling you to and the needs they have. How can you look closely at and understand their situation and their needs? How can you keep a compassionate posture toward them?
* As you consider the context and the people, what hospitality can you provide? What can you not provide? Consider the realistic limitations of time, energy, resources, and commitment.
* What clarity do you need to offer those in your context? What has remained unsaid? What needs to be said?
* How can you clarify and still keep the purpose of hospitality and welcome within your context?

Humility, conviction, and compassion serve as needed boundaries. We need these qualities to serve others and continue in a posture of welcome and hospitality.

10

SPACIOUS GUIDANCE

Bright yellow arrows met me along the way. As I walked the well-guided pilgrimage path of the Camino de Santiago in Spain, I received the gifts of spaciousness via road markers. Millions have walked the Camino before me; for them, like me, its spacious guidance made way for freedom, security, and pauses, all at an undemanding pace. Each pilgrim had a different purpose for walking the Camino, but our path was the same. Even as I began the Camino with my own distinct purpose, I imagined the thousands who had walked before me. The thought brought me a sense of community and solidarity with those before me. I was not the first, nor would I be the last. Along with others, I was embraced by the communion of saints: I knew this path had been walked, was being walked, and would be walked. The Camino gave me both spaciousness and guidance, both through literal markers on the path and through communal connection. As I walked my own internal journey, we walked the external journey together. Even as I walked on my own, I was never alone.

The path itself provided hospitality, and so did many people. My group leaders spent months of preparation on details to cultivate space for our souls. We had Zoom calls, packing lists, training recommendations, and more. In addition to the hosting group, my workplace made way for the journey to be a part of my life and to serve others in the future. My family marked the calendar with the dates I would be gone, and my husband cared for both work and home while I was away. Many others advised me with their wisdom and training tips. The Camino and the communion of saints, past, present, and future, provided the hospitality of spacious guidance on this journey of faith.

As someone who likes to blaze a trail, I found welcome and respite in the well-worn path. Others blazed the trail so that many could walk in it. The hospitality of people and the hospitality of the Camino markers gave us space to journey and explore, but it also guided us to keep us from being lost, hurt, or too far off the path.

LIFE INSIDE THE MARKERS

Markers are a crucial part of any journey. Driving on a highway, we see mile markers; walking along a hiking trail, we see directional signs. We have markers in Scripture that give us spacious paths to walk in—ways to live that bring life. They also give us security and guidance, helping us stay on good paths. These markers were created by people who know the way, see the way, and have worked to prepare future travelers on the journey. God gave the Israelites the Ten Commandments for security and guidance. Each command serves as a marker pointing to the path for us to walk by. The Ten Commandments show us the way that brings life and gives others life through us. They give us the compass to guide our walk and the spaciousness to live good lives in the world God has called us to.

Though some might see these markers of guidance as reassuring, others see them (and have experienced them) as restrictive. These markers are meant to provide freedom, yet many have added to them, unnecessarily confining the way. When preaching to the crowds and his disciples, Jesus speaks to this issue. He says that the teachers of the law sit on high and not only demand the commandments be met, but they add to them. Worse, these teachers don't even do the extras they require (Matthew 23:1-4). Have you ever experienced when someone demands more of you than they are willing to do themselves? They are keeping up an image of looking good and righteous, but in truth, they are anything but. Jesus directly condemns this hypocrisy, clarifying that these commandments are markers of life and freedom rather than extra burdens (Matthew 23:4). Markers are reassurance that we are on the good path that leads to life.

DECREASED ANXIETY

During my doctoral research on hospitality, I asked interviewees, "What helps you to be a good guest?" Eight out of ten people answered by citing clear expectations of time and space. They wanted to know which bedroom was theirs, what food they could eat, and when the hosts were expecting meals together. When I asked why this was important, they each said that clarity of expectations and guidelines as guests decreased their anxiety about where they could and couldn't go, what they could use, and what was set apart for them. These things provided markers for enjoying their time as a guest. Christine Pohl says, "Sometimes welcome must be limited and distinctions made, however, if only for the sake of other guests or members already within the community. The amount of space available and the physical and emotional capacity of the hosts and guests impose certain limits." For the guests I interviewed, knowing these guidelines allowed them the freedom to enjoy being guests.

On the Digital Silent Retreats I convene, we limit the number of participants per host. We do this because a host can only attentively listen to so many people; visually, when a Zoom room gets larger than nine persons, the participants get lost on the screen, and the guests also need more attention. In creating this limitation, we are honoring the host's capacity, the guests' needs, and the retreat's purpose: to create brave and protected spaces for people to meet with God and one another for the sake of the world. As registrations have increased, we have added hosts and used breakout rooms to keep the ratio small, guarding our guests and keeping our purpose. When our markers were being pressed against, we had to reevaluate what we could do. We could choose to restrict people from entering or adapt our guidelines while staying aligned with our purpose. We decided to adapt our guidelines. Guidelines have a purpose; they can be moved if doing so benefits the guest and aligns with the purpose. They aren't designed to restrict, but to create space.

Guidelines can be reassuring when used well, but can feel restrictive when not. In Matthew 23, Jesus remarks on how the religious leaders had made the Law of Moses into heavy burdens—burdens these leaders weren't even willing to carry. God's welcome to life had become a weight to bear rather than a spacious framework to live within.

Rather than mimicking the religious leaders, how can we create welcoming spaces, keep markers in their place, and invite others to live inside them? We do this through generous authority and the gift of limitations.

GENEROUS AUTHORITY

In March of 2020, everyone was figuring out how to shelter in place and stop a worldwide pandemic from spreading and taking more lives. While we were figuring out what it meant to stay home and go outside only when we needed and were allowed to, we were figuring out how to educate children, work from home, and find the necessities to live by. Churches fumbled through worshiping and practicing community when they could not gather. Along with many others, I struggled to know how to spend time with God—with all the distractions and scattered schedules, time seemed to slip away. I wondered if I might go about addressing struggle for myself and others.

Acting on this curiosity, the Digital Silent Retreats were created. I invited my small email list to join online one Saturday morning for three hours of retreat. People joined from their homes, the park, their closet, and any quiet space they could find. We gathered on Zoom with introductions, guidelines for the retreat, and a retreat guide, and I introduced them to a spiritual practice. They were then released to spend ninety minutes with God in solitude and silence, guided along the way by the retreat set of practices. They were free to go at the pace they needed, in step with the Spirit. After ninety minutes, they were to return to Zoom, and we would share what came up during the solitude and silence time. The power of this last hour surprised me. I had created the retreat for people to meet with God. Little did I realize that this time would provide communal connection, testimony, encouragement, and solidarity. We needed one another, and this time gave us to each other.

I continued the retreats the next month, and the next. Each month, they gave us a framework and spaciousness. This spacious guidance is one of the pillars of these Digital Silent Retreats; it is a key part of what the hosts offer. These retreats continue today. They provide spacious guidance for candor and courage, freedom and breakthrough, community and connection.

Gathering guru Priya Parker says,

A gathering run on generous authority is run with a strong, confident hand, but it is run selflessly, for the sake of others. Generous authority is imposing in a way that serves your guests. The way a host practices generous authority is through protecting guests, equalizing guests, and connecting guests to one another.

Generous authority is at the heart of hosting. Markers create a framework, serving the guest, stranger, family, and friend, giving them the assurance of the space we provide for them.

THE GIFT OF LIMITATIONS

We can also provide spacious guidance through markers of our limitations. I witnessed this once when I saw author Katherine Wolf preaching the goodness of God from a wheelchair. As she went on stage, the congregation watched her being guided up the stairs while another took her wheelchair up. We had to wait for her to settle, wondering whether her wheelchair was locked.

I had never seen or heard a sermon from someone whose sufferings were evident and who wrestled hope for herself and others. When Katherine stood up from her physical wheelchair to talk about our invisible wheelchairs, we all leaned in even more.

Katherine and her husband Jay have suffered, living with disability, seeking hope, and leaning into life. As she shared their story on the stage, she fully embodied living life from her limitations, her dependence, and her vulnerability. She shared about the things in her life that gave her the way forward in her faith. She learned these hopeful and faithful ways of living from the life of Jesus and her own circumstances, and she guided us on how to walk within them. What she shared reminded me what markers make possible: spaciousness, pathways, guidance, creativity, and hope. She brought hospitality to a stage that, ironically, she could not reach on her own—communicating to us that we cannot live on our own. In her limitations, she brought us the limitless hope of Jesus, who gave us a way to walk in and pointed us to the markers along the way. Life had forced her to choose whether she would see her path as spacious or restrictive, and she taught us how to accept limitations as markers that could still lead to a good and spacious life. She chose spaciousness within her profound suffering and life limitations.

I have no idea how much it takes for Katherine, her husband, and her family to be present with others. I don't know if Katherine has been told she has the gift of hospitality, but I do know that hospitality showed up that day in a wheelchair. Her words created a spacious path to journey in our sufferings, giving us hope despite all of our limitations.

PUSHING THE LIMITS

Few phrases raise my rage like "Stay in your lane." This phrase has often been used to promote acceptance and stagnation. Often it is used to control us, rather than help us think carefully about our limitations. We can always learn within our limits, but sometimes we need to challenge these limits with humility and curiosity. Katherine and Jay Wolf have not thrown in the towel to accept her physical limitations. In their book *Suffer Strong*, the Wolfs describe their journey of healing, work, and strengthening. We need discernment to accept limitations and live into them without living a life of stagnation and defeat. We need others to help us know when to push and when to accept.

On the Camino, my friend Angela helped me in just this way. We were walking together on the last day, just miles from Santiago. As we drew near, it seemed like the miles kept extending farther. We questioned the truth of the trail markers; our weariness and achy joints were yelling. We were both glad we had each other as the journey was longer than expected. We would take turns doubting the legitimacy of the markers and would reassure each other to keep going.

We often need others to help us know when to push the limits and when to accept them. And it is good to have people of wisdom with us to help us in those times.

NAMING THE MARKERS

Our markers provide the pathway for growing in hospitality and offering it to others. I have named a few markers for life's journey, such as the Ten Commandments, the realities of limitations, and the path provided in community. These markers guide, humble, and strengthen us to continue following Jesus and inviting others to the spacious path he offers.

Through our life markers, we can remind others of the good markers around them. What we have learned and how we have been provided for and strengthened, give us compassion, care, and awareness. When we do these faithfully, our spaciousness grows deeper and wider as we travel with instructions, limitations, and stories.

The Spiritual Practice of Examen

When we learn to walk our path within a spacious framework, we are more likely to be able to discern frameworks with others and make way for them to experience spaciousness.

One spiritual practice that allows us to discern the path and walk in it is the practice of examen. Saint Ignatius of Loyola proposed a form of the examen over four hundred years ago. This practice is a prayerful reflection on the events of the day to "detect God's presence and to discern his direction for us."

Various questions can help us detect God's presence and discern his direction. Examen questions are included at the beginning and end of the day. Through this practice, you will be invited to a three-part framework. You will use a commandment as a guidepost, then receive the spaciousness it provides. Throughout, you'll notice moments when you want to push on the markers.

Ideally, commit to this practice for ten to fourteen days. If you cannot commit to this timeframe, try to at least use the practice three to four times in one week. Write your responses in a notebook or journal. The repetition of the practice, along with preserving your responses, will allow you to see any patterns, echoes, or contrasts between your responses each day.

Morning Examen

In prayer, ask God which commandment will be a guidepost for you today. There are many commands in Scripture, but for the sake of this exercise, choose one of the Ten Commandments.

You can use this abbreviated version of the Ten Commandments, paraphrased from Exodus 20:3-17:

You shall have no other gods before me.

You shall not make for yourself a carved image, or any likeness of anything that is in heaven above, or that is in the earth beneath, or that is in the water under the earth. You shall not bow down to them or serve them.

You shall not take the name of the Lord your God in vain.

Remember the Sabbath day, to keep it holy.

Honor your father and your mother.

You shall not murder.

You shall not commit adultery.

You shall not steal.

You shall not bear false witness against your neighbor.

You shall not covet anything that is your neighbor's.

* Which commandment will you focus on? Try to keep this consistent for a few days.
* As you focus on the single commandment, try not to add to or diminish it. Keep it simple and straightforward.
* In prayer, ask the Spirit to help you honor the commandment that day as it is meant to be.
* Throughout your day, remind yourself of the commandment, noticing how often you are tempted to live outside of its marker.

Evening Examen

* What was it like having the commandment as a marker in your day?
* How did the commandment provide guidance and spaciousness today?
* Where were you tempted to go outside the marker?
* Through today's marker, how is God inviting you to live?

11

CLOSINGS AND BEGINNINGS

MY FATHER'S LAST WORDS will stay with me forever. Not only will his words stay with me, so will the room, environment, and emotions of that moment. Last words have lasting power; they can be a gift that brings us growth or a curse that haunts us. Researchers Chip and Dan Heath write in their book *The Power of Moments* that the ending of an event or gathering is one of the key moments in which a person determines the value and meaning of their experience. Think of the end of a relationship, the death of a dream, the closing act of a performance, and even the last deal in a business—endings are powerful. In these endings we have the chance for gracious closure, allowing hospitality to finish its good work and preparing us for new, good work to begin.

The book of Acts records Jesus' last words to his disciples. I can imagine these last words lingered throughout the disciples' lives and ministries. When they asked if Jesus had returned for the ultimate and final restoration of all things, he responded this way: "It is not for you to know the times or dates the Father has set by his own authority. But you will receive power when the Holy Spirit comes on you; and you will be my witnesses in Jerusalem, and in all Judea and Samaria, and to the ends of the earth" (Acts 1:6-8).

In other words, he told them, "You don't and can't know the information you long for. But the Father knows. And you will receive what you need for the work you are called to." As Jesus finished his physical time on earth, he didn't give them the information they longed for but the blessing they needed. His disciples needed a promise that would anchor the good work they were called to. This ending brought the opportunity for a new beginning, which was necessary for the good work to come. And Jesus blessed it.

Endings bring the opportunity for blessing—blessing people and their work, speaking hopefulness into the future. And sometimes endings need repair. Since endings are deeply attached to relational dynamics, we need to understand what it takes to create a hospitable ending that gives everyone a new way of moving forward.

This hospitable ending is the work of closing, or closure. We cannot always close things completely, but we can work with intention and courage to repair.

It would be good to pause and further distinguish between a closing and an ending here. Endings are often clear. A job loss, a death, or a move to another city is clear. One thing has ended, and another is beginning. Closings are the work of endings. They are the goodbyes of endings. Closing is working to repair, transition, grieve, and heal in response to an ending. To close well requires intention and courage. Closings may come while something is ending, or they may begin after an ending. For example, my friends whose family members have had dementia began their closings before the end of their loved ones' lives. In contrast, friends who suddenly lost someone cannot start their closing until after the unexpected death.

Good closings make ways for new beginnings. And part of the work of hospitality is leaning into these closings.

ALL IN

"It's not just your family. You are all loud." This was my husband's response after spending time with one of our Armenian friends.

Yes, to speak Armenian, your volume must increase. Armenians are passionate, expressive, and full of emotion. We are creative and intuitive and, due to our history, we have learned to be survivors. We vigorously discuss both inconsequential details and the most important matters. To be Armenian means to have a robust internal world and be outwardly expressive. Growing up, this characteristic was overwhelming to me, a highly sensitive person absorbing all the emotions, expressions, and words around me. I often retreated from the intensity of the environment. To this day, some of my family members prefer the expressiveness of Pentecostalism while I remain a Presbyterian minister.

Different expressions aside, the gift of this side of our culture is that we are all in from beginning to end. We are committed and loyal, staying with you no matter what. My mom never left my dad while he was in hospice. She didn't retreat from the pain of watching her loved one die. Each child remained near our dad and leaned in until the end. Because we were all in, we could listen and be present to our final experiences and words with our dad. And we had the gift of time with him, even though we only knew about his cancer for a few months.

My memory is filled not only with last words but also with our many last times together: the last time we went to a toy store so he could buy gifts for his grandkids, the last Tex-Mex meal he could enjoy before his body couldn't take food, the last picture, and the last smiles. He had the opportunity to give us his last wishes, and we have kept those as we have been able. We leaned into this closing season, and because of it, we were able to love and be loved to the very end.

Committing all the way to the end is not easy. We often want to avoid difficult moments or awkward conversations. We make excuses for why we didn't go, and then we regret that we didn't show up. But closings are about showing up. And they are hard and worthy work.

The option to be all in at the end is also a privilege. We have all had to deal with endings we didn't see coming, last times that we never dreamed of, and goodbyes that couldn't be communicated. Some of us have been prevented from being all in by financial or physical limitations. We need the greatest grace for circumstances like these. And God has provided some creative means of closure. Friends have told me about receiving closure through dreams dreamed and stories heard, goodbyes that have come through memories of forgotten moments. We can still be all in, as long as we are all in what God might have for us.

This is who God is. God is a God of closings that make way for beginnings, bringing new life from death. And new life is a place of celebration and welcome. He is a God of repair and restoration, redemption and hope. Just as God calls us to be all in, God is all in before we could be. He knows the beginning, the end, and the beginning again. And God is with us through it all. Let's see him walk with one person through endings and beginnings.

NECESSARY REPAIR

The Gospel of John devotes time to the restoration of the disciple Peter. Peter had not been present for Jesus' death. He had been hiding out of fear, consumed by shame from denying he knew Jesus. Peter turned to self-protection; he took physical and emotional cover as Jesus was being taken to his public crucifixion (John 18:15-27). Peter was absent at the end—anything but all in. Even so, the risen Jesus makes a point to minister to Peter and repair what was broken.

After his resurrection, Jesus meets some of his disciples on the beach. He serves them food and, after eating, asks Simon Peter about his love for him. Jesus asks him three times, Peter responds affirmatively three times, and Jesus instructs Peter three times to care for his sheep. Finally, Jesus tells Peter what death will be like for him and renews his call for Peter to follow him (John 21:15-19).

In the same breath that Jesus invites Peter to restored life and calling, he foretells Peter's end. The moment is an ending within an ending, a closing that makes way for a new life that will also end. This is the cycle of beginnings and endings, and the good work in the middle.

Jesus showed up all in. After his resurrection, he moved toward Peter, restoring their relationship and Peter's call. He also showed up to Mary in the garden, and he showed up to the disciples in the upper room as they hid (John 20:11-17, 19-20). He provided what was needed in each situation, and he called his friends to purpose and contribution. Jesus shows up with great grace, inviting us to join in the feast of relationship both present and future. This is what repair and closings do. This is what hospitality does.

For years, I served as one of the pastors of a beautiful congregation. This congregation witnessed several significant milestones in my life: the birth of my children, my ordination, the death of my father, and many more. This congregation had gone through transition; new life was emerging as a new senior pastor was called to lead them. Part of my time there was spent under the new pastor's leadership and the culture he created. Over time, I grew quite weary. There was the work that was in my job description, and then there was the work that was not in my job description. The job description was fruitful and exciting. The unwritten job description was discouraging and frustrating. I grew exhausted and longed to be able to leave.

God graciously released me from the work, and as I pressed into discerning God's voice of release, I also pressed into honest and hard conversations with senior leaders. The senior leaders and I leaned into ending my time there with meaningful closure. I am so grateful for the intentionality of all parties, as I know this is not the story for many leaders. Later, from time to time, I would return to the church for denominational meetings or to work from the new and beautiful space that the leadership had created. Any time I saw the senior pastor, he always moved toward me. Once, he heard my voice in the hallway and stopped his studies in the library to come out and say hi. He would ask if I needed anything; he would welcome me in a crowd. Each time he moved toward me, he was doing the work of relational repair.

I remember one time when our denomination was worshiping in the sanctuary. At Communion, my husband and I walked forward to receive. I chose to join the shorter line because this senior pastor was in the front row, and I wanted to tell him what a good place the church was. He was sitting down, and as I got closer, he saw me and stood up. (I thought I was making this idea up, but my husband confirmed that he stood up because he saw me coming.) When I passed him by, he was ready with his arms out for a hug. I told him, "This is such a good place. A good, good place." I hope that as he was leaning into repair, he knew that I was also leaning into it. We were working toward a shared goal of wholeness, kindness, courage, and care.

Sadly, I will never know. He unexpectedly died of natural causes one month later. I now sit writing this chapter from the same sanctuary, with a view of the last place where we exchanged words, repair, and care.

Repair is part of our good work, both when we receive and when we give it. We do this good, hospitable work because Jesus does it. We do this work because when we choose to close well, we begin well. And with endings, there is always a beginning to come. What a grace it is when we can repair before an ending.

I imagine this is not the story of all who read this book. You may long for restoration and closing in a particular situation, but the opportunity has passed or seems impossible. God continues to be a God of restoration and repair. Allow him to give you what you need for your journey ahead.

CLOSING THE LOOP

My dear café-owning Aussie friends, who I introduced in an earlier chapter, continue to spread their hospitality as they provide places of respite. They began their work with the goal of three coffee shops, and they are now up to five, with more on the way. These brothers are the most unassuming men you will meet. They carry kindness and warmth wherever they go, serving great coffee and providing beautiful opportunities for human connection. Through their posture and presence, they have created an incredibly hospitable space.

One day, I told them how great their hospitality was and how wonderful I feel when I come in. I asked one brother for the specifics of how they create this remarkable atmosphere. When he walked me through their training, I was struck by their practice of "closing the loop." He shared that the goal is for everyone who comes in to be thanked personally, handed their drinks, and given a personal goodbye as they walk out the door. They make no distinctions between the guests who dash in for five seconds to pick up an order and the guests who stay for fifty minutes with a friend. (They even care for the Freddie freeloaders!) The thank-you and goodbye matter—for every person. As we talked further, we agreed that being thanked on the way out leads to a powerful ending interaction. This ending leaves the person with a lingering sense of being cared for, noticed, and appreciated; this closing sense paves the way for a guest to return. Even as a brilliant businessperson, this brother's care is genuine. His business model includes closing the loop, which expresses profound care.

We can close the loop in a million different ways. Whether it's by walking someone to the door as they leave or by sending an appreciative follow-up email or text, we can provide warmth and care through closure. Such closure will allow for more beginnings to come.

Closings are a significant part of our endings; they make way for new beginnings, especially through repair. This repair opens opportunities for connection, love, and creativity. Closings aren't easy, but they are worth it. Endings matter, and they matter for new beginnings.

The Spiritual Practice of Confession and Assurance of Grace

How can we cultivate a posture of being all in to our closings and intentional about the places of repair we extend? For this, we will turn to the spiritual practice of confession and the assurance of grace. This practice might seem like an odd one—hang in there with me.

Confession is a spiritual practice that comes with many opinions and experiences. People disagree on whether it is needed, and many have experienced shame and harm through it. You may have an image popping up in your mind as you read. If you have a negative picture of confession, I invite you to consider it as a spiritual practice with surprising and consistent freedom on the other side. And our confessions are very near to us—so near that we don't speak of them to many people or share the freedom coming from them. Yet regularly practicing confession and being reminded of God's grace and pardon allow us to walk in a strange and surprising freedom.

For over five years, I wrote corporate confessions for our worshiping community, as required by our weekly service liturgy. Each week, I sat with a Scripture text before me and a congregation in mind to pen words that might create space for lives to be opened up to God. I cannot say that anyone ever praised the confessions each week. (Admittedly, they also didn't know I wrote them.) No one ever said they were wowed or moved by our confessional practice. Yet I hope that God met them and that they were able to receive grace and assurance of their forgiveness.

So why is confession tied to hospitable closings? Closings allow us to reflect on what we have said and done, and what we have left unsaid and undone. Closings are often ripe for regret. And shame lives quite near to regret. This combination of reflection, regret, and shame can lead to withdrawal, in which we avoid the hard work of ending well. Confession allows us to face these reflections with courage and confidence because of Jesus' forgiveness and grace. When we allow our sin to be met by the Savior, he strengthens us to lean into our closings. So, practicing confession allows us to come out of hiding, step away from the shame we have carried, and place our regrets before Jesus. Sometimes we need to confess sins against others. Sometimes we confess sins against God. And often, we need to confess sins against ourselves. Confession is an opportunity to acknowledge anything that is not aligned with God's good, beautiful, and life-giving ways.

We can walk into confession knowing we are forgiven, because Jesus promised this. We absorb the truth of the grace and freedom that Jesus has for us, and we walk out of it in greater freedom—freedom to love well to the end. We receive an opportunity just like the one Jesus gave Peter: the chance for repair, restoration, and possibility, coming with confession and an assurance of grace.

How might we practice and journey through confession toward this freedom to love?

Confess to a Trusted Friend

Consider confessing to a trusted friend who can reflect Jesus' voice and words back to you. James instructs us, saying, "Therefore confess your sins to each other and pray for each other so that you may be healed. The prayer of a righteous person is powerful and effective" (James 5:16).

Spend some time in prayer, asking God for anything he wants to bring to your attention. If it is helpful, consider using confessions written by others. Share your confession with another, asking them to assure you of God's forgiveness. There is something powerful that another person can offer when they hold our most vulnerable selves and love us through prayer. According to James, that power can heal us. When we are healed, we can hold others and walk through closings with them. And healed endings lead to beautiful beginnings.

Confess to Jesus

Consider imagining yourself in the context of Jesus and Peter in John 21. Imagine that you are Peter, and Jesus is inviting you to restoration. As you imagine yourself with Jesus, place your trust in his voice of love, restoration, and calling.

As you sit with Jesus, rest in the assurance of his grace:

> The LORD is compassionate and gracious,
> > slow to anger, abounding in love.
> He will not always accuse,
> > nor will he harbor his anger forever;
> he does not treat us as our sins deserve
> > or repay us according to our iniquities.
> For as high as the heavens are above the earth,
> > so great is his love for those who fear him;
> as far as the east is from the west,
> > so far has he removed our transgressions from us.
>
> As a father has compassion on his children,
> > so the LORD has compassion on those who fear him;
> for he knows how we are formed,
> > he remembers that we are dust. (Psalm 103:8-14)

CONCLUSION

HOSPITALITY COMES FROM PEOPLE, not just places. It is a practice that becomes a posture, which we can carry wherever we go. We can provide welcome to stranger and friend alike. With the creativity of hospitality, we expand our definitions, taking welcome to both familiar and foreign places. As we carry hospitality to the world, we remember that God first carried welcome to us.

We can be people of welcome, because God always welcomes us.

We can be people who look at and see others, because God looks at and sees us.

We can be people who are always at home, because God is this home for us.

And our world needs welcome. Our world needs those who look and see. It needs people who provide places of home.

We can always find our home in God. And our world needs reminders that we can always come home. God consistently welcomes us home, whether he walks toward us or we walk toward him. May we become people who carry welcome wherever we go and help others find their home in God.

ACKNOWLEDGMENTS

GOD EXTENDS HIS HOSPITALITY EVERYWHERE, if we would only look and see. Hospitality has been offered to me throughout my life, by family, friends, countries, living rooms, churches, coffee shops, conversations, creation, and more. Each of these people and places have been gifts of grace.

I am grateful that I can see God's abundant welcome toward me. It is a near-impossible task to name and include all the people and places that have made way for this book, so I will refrain from specificities. Thank you to all who have looked for and seen me, and to all who have held and strengthened me with next steps. Thank you to those who continue to show me the great generosity and welcome of friendship and love. May we each carry God's expansive and multiplying welcome into the world.

QUESTIONS FOR REFLECTION AND DISCUSSION

THE FOLLOWING QUESTIONS are an option for small group discussion. Consider them after you have read and engaged with the spiritual practices. Each session includes two chapters and can be taken at the pace your group needs. You do not need to answer every question.

I encourage you to use the questions that are most helpful for your learning and discussion. Follow the energy of your group's learning and conversation. Give space for each person to engage and have time to share.

SESSION 1: CHAPTERS 1–2

1. What stood out to you from the reading and practices?
2. What mirrors in your life can help you redefine hospitality?
3. How do you resist these mirrors?
4. How do you welcome them?
5. What is it like to consider hospitality as a posture in addition to a place?
6. What contexts in your life feel clear to you?

7. What contexts in your life are surprising to you?

8. Who has been an illuminator in your life?

9. What do you most want to work on in the work of listening?

SESSION 2: CHAPTERS 3-4

1. What stood out to you from the reading and practices?

2. What is it like to consider God as the first host?

3. How does thinking about God as the first host shift how you see yourself?

4. What did your self-assessment on the hospitality scale reveal to you?

5. How can God's persistent welcome invite you to regularly receive from him?

6. Have you experienced a time when you were initially welcomed, but found the welcome wearing off? What was this like?

7. Have you ever had to stay in an inhospitable space? Who was there with you during that time? What did their presence provide for you?

8. Where does Jesus want you to remain and receive? How will you do so?

SESSION 3: CHAPTERS 5-6

1. What stood out to you from the reading and practices?

2. How do you most resist Jesus? In what ways? Consider the trio of hurt:

   * Hiding

   * Hardness of heart

  * Hurt heart

3. Who do you most resist welcome from? Why?

   * Jesus

   * Yourself

   * Community

4. What part of yourself do you need to welcome, empathize with, and be non-judgmental with?

5. Think of a time when you thought you'd be the giver, but ended up receiving. What was that like?

6. How do you keep a ledger of hospitality?

7. Have you experienced the exchange of gifts described in the chapter? How so?

8. Do you need others for any hard thing you are walking through? Who can you ask to walk with you?

SESSION 4: CHAPTERS 7–8

1. How has preparation helped you be present to the unexpected?

2. What attachments bind you?

3. Of the following ways of life, which one do you want to lean into? How will you do so?

   * Surrendering power and trusting the Spirit

   * Slowing down and finding security in Jesus

   * Preparing and practicing

4. Which of the stories and Scriptures most resonated with you and why?

5. When has the work of welcome and hospitality cost you greatly? If God hasn't already, how might he restore you?

6. How can you cultivate vision for being a person of welcome and hospitality?

SESSION 5: CHAPTERS 9–10

1. What stood out to you from the reading and practices?

2. When have you experienced a hidden boundary? What was that like?

3. When have you seen the clarity of a boundary serve a community?

4. When have you experienced a boundary that helped with compassion? What was that like?

5. When have you seen markers that have been helpful along the way?

6. What extra requirements do you associate with hospitality?

7. How do you tend to respond to limitations?

8. Who do you need to help you discern whether to push on limitations or accept them?

SESSION 6: CHAPTER 11 AND CONCLUSION

1. What stood out to you from the reading and practices?

2. How have you experienced good endings?

3. Are there any endings you wish would have gone differently?

4. What role does confession play in your life? How might it play a more ordinary role?

5. Are you anticipating any endings in your life? How might you lean into ending well?

6. What new things will you lean into as a person of welcome?

NOTES

1. THE POSTURE YOU TAKE

7 *Posture of hospitality*: Jude Tiersma-Watson, "Jude Tiersma-Watson on Hospitality," October 10, 2016, Fuller Studio, YouTube Video, 00:35–00:55, www.youtube.com/watch?v=Qyr-E4PraAk.

10 *"There was never an assumption"*: Christine Pohl, *Making Room: Recovering Hospitality as Christian Tradition* (Grand Rapids, MI: Eerdmans, 1999), 41.

2. THE PLACES YOU ARE

21 *"Hospitality does not entail"*: Amy Oden, *And You Welcomed Me: A Sourcebook on Hospitality in Early Christianity* (Nashville: Abingdon Press, 2001), 109.

26 *"bigger, respected, and lit up"*: David Brooks, "The Essential Skills for Being Human," *New York Times*, October 19, 2023, www.nytimes.com /2023/10/19/opinion/social-skills-connection.html.

27 *"Stories open doors"*: Eugene Peterson, *Christ in Ten Thousand Places: A Conversation in Spiritual Theology* (Grand Rapids, MI: Eerdmans, 2008), 19.

3. THE FIRST HOST

30 *"The larger spiritual context"*: Amy Oden, *And You Welcomed Me: A Sourcebook on Hospitality in Early Christianity* (Nashville: Abingdon Press, 2001), 86-87.

37 *"Hospitality is at the heart"*: Christine Pohl, *Living into Community: Cultivating Practices that Sustain Us* (Grand Rapids, MI: Eerdmans, 2011), 159.

4. COUNTERFEIT HOSPITALITY

41 *"Fitting in is about assessing"*: Brené Brown, *The Gifts of Imperfection: Let Go of Who You Think You're Supposed to Be and Embrace Who You Are* (Danvers, MA: Hazelden Publishing, 2010), 145.

44   *A phenomenon called "ghosting"*: "Ghosting," Psychology Today (website), accessed January 7, 2025, www.psychologytoday.com/us/basics/ghosting.

5. HEALED HEARTS ARE HOSPITABLE HEARTS

54   *"Deep sensitivity"*: Christine Pohl, *Making Room: Recovering Hospitality as a Christian Tradition* (Grand Rapids, MI: Eerdmans, 1999), 65.

56   *"The fact that the townspeople"*: Lynn Cohick, "The 'Woman at the Well': Was the Samaritan Woman Really an Adulteress?" *Kregel Academic Blog*, March 22, 2024, https://kregelacademicblog.com/biblical-studies/the -woman-at-the-well-was-the-samaritan-woman-really-an-adulteress. Blog post based on Sandra Glahn, ed., *Vindicating the Vixens* (Grand Rapids, MI: Kregel Academic, 2017), chap. 12.

57   *Someone to come and find us:* "Curt Thompson and the Soul of Shame," November 21, 2019, in *The Faith and Work Podcast,* season 4, episode 4, www.denverinstitute.org/s4e4-curt-thompson-soul-shame/.

58   *"A hard heart usually starts"*: Katherine and Jay Wolf, *Suffer Strong* (Nashville: Thomas Nelson, 2020), 135.

6. THE EXCHANGE OF GIFTS

66   *"Because the guest"*: Amy Oden, *And You Welcomed Me: A Sourcebook on Hospitality in Early Christianity* (Nashville: Abingdon Press, 2001), 51.

68   *"The brain can do"*: Curt Thompson, "Neuroplasticity," April 6, 2021, on *Being Known,* podcast, S1E8, 58:48–1:02:53, https://podcasts.apple.com /us/podcast/being-known-podcast/id1556261828?i=1000516060392.

7. PREPARING YOURSELF

75   *"One of the hardest things"*: Parker Palmer, *Let Your Life Speak: Listening for the Voice of Vocation* (San Francisco: Josey-Bass, 2000), 63.

79   *"The real 'work' of prayer"*: Henri Nouwen, *Life of the Beloved: Spiritual Living in a Secular World*, 10th anniv. ed. (PublishDrive, 2002), 75–76.

8. CULTIVATING VISION

87   *Legacy Sites:* Learn more about the work of the Equal Justice Initiative at https://eji.org/about/.

9. NECESSARY BOUNDARIES

93   *"By definition, hospitality"*: Christine Pohl, *Making Room: Recovering Hospitality as a Christian Tradition* (Grand Rapids, MI: Eerdmans, 1999), 129.

97 *"Predictable and consistent boundaries"*: Caroline Westerhoff, *Good Fences: The Boundaries of Hospitality* (Harrisburg, PA: Morehouse Publishing, 2004), 90.

10. SPACIOUS GUIDANCE

105 *"Sometimes welcome must be limited"*: Christine Pohl, *Making Room: Recovering Hospitality as Christian Tradition* (Grand Rapids, MI: Eerdmans, 1999), 130.

108 *"A gathering run on generous authority"*: Priya Parker, *The Art of Gathering: How We Meet and Why It Matters* (New York: Riverhead Books, 2020), 81-94.

Katherine and her husband Jay: To learn more about their work, visit the Hope Heals website at www.hopeheals.com.

109 *The Wolfs describe their journey*: See Katherine and Jay Wolf, *Suffer Strong: How to Survive Anything by Redefining Everything* (Grand Rapids, MI: Zondervan, 2020), 19-36, 163-78.

111 *"Detect God's presence"*: "How Can I Pray?" Ignatian Spirituality (website), Loyola Press, accessed January 11, 2025, www.ignatianspirituality.com /ignatian-prayer/the-examen/how-can-i-pray.

11. CLOSINGS AND BEGINNINGS

113 *The ending of an event or gathering*: Chip and Dan Heath, *The Power of Moments: Why Certain Experiences Have Extraordinary Impact* (New York: Simon and Schuster, 2017), 8.

IVP formatio

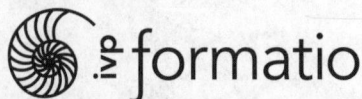